The Protestant Ethic Debate

STUDIES IN SOCIAL AND POLITICAL THOUGHT
Editor: Gerald Delanty, *University of Liverpool*

This series publishes peer-reviewed scholarly books on all aspects of social and political thought. It will be of interest to scholars and advanced students working in the areas of social theory and sociology, the history of ideas, philosophy, political and legal theory, anthropological and cultural theory. Works of individual scholarship will have preference for inclusion in the series, but appropriate co- or multi-authored works and edited volumes of outstanding quality or exceptional merit will also be included. The series will also consider English translations of major works in other languages.

Challenging and intellectually innovative books are particularly welcome on the history of social and political theory; modernity and the social and human sciences; major historical or contemporary thinkers; the philosophy of the social sciences; theoretical issues on the transformation of contemporary society; social change and European societies.

It is not series policy to publish textbooks, research reports, empirical case studies, conference proceedings or books of an essayist or polemical nature.

Discourse and Knowledge: The Making of Enlightenment Sociology
Piet Strydom

Social Theory after the Holocaust
edited by Robert Fine and Charles Turner

The Moment: Time and Rupture in Modern Thought
edited by Heidrun Friese

Essaying Montaigne
John O'Neill

The Protestant Ethic Debate: Max Weber's Replies to his Critics, 1907–1910
edited by David Chalcraft and Austin Harrington
translated by Austin Harrington and Mary Shields

The Protestant Ethic Debate

Max Weber's Replies to his Critics, 1907–1910

Edited by
DAVID J. CHALCRAFT
and AUSTIN HARRINGTON

Translated by
AUSTIN HARRINGTON
and MARY SHIELDS

LIVERPOOL UNIVERSITY PRESS

First published 2001 by
LIVERPOOL UNIVERSITY PRESS
4 Cambridge Street
Liverpool
L69 7ZU

British Library Cataloguing-in-Publication Data
A British Library CIP record is available

ISBN 0 85323 976 2 cased
     0 85323 968 X paperback

Typeset by Northern Phototypesetting Co Ltd, Bolton
Printed in Great Britain by Bell and Bain Ltd, Glasgow

Contents

Acknowledgements

This project began life in the Sociology Unit at Oxford Brookes University in 1994. Mary Shields was appointed Research Assistant to work alongside David Chalcraft (Project Director and General Editor) on producing a translation and critical edition of Weber's replies to his critics. Mary and David would like to thank the sociology staff at Oxford Brookes for their financial and moral support for the project, in particular Frank Webster (now at the University of Birmingham). The project then moved to the University of Derby in 1996 when David Chalcraft was appointed Head of Sociology. Mary Shields continued to work on the project on a freelance basis and we were joined in 1998 by Austin Harrington (now at the University of Leeds) for the final two years of the work. Austin Harrington and Mary Shields were funded by the School of Education and Social Science at the University of Derby and we are grateful to the School for its financial support and interest in the project. The responsibility for the translation lies solely with Austin Harrington and Mary Shields, with the occasional query and prompting from David Chalcraft. The Introduction was solely written by David Chalcraft. Austin Harrington is responsible for the summaries of the reviews of Weber's text by Karl Fischer and Felix Rachfahl and for most of the editors' footnotes, as well as the translators' note and other editorial matters. Mary Shields provided working translations of other important texts and spent time in Oxford libraries researching literary, linguistic, bibliographical and biographical details that have helped with the construction of parts of the Introduction. We are grateful to Professor Gerard Delanty for offering to publish the volume in his Studies in Social and Political Thought series and we want to register our appreciation of his patient support in seeing the project through to publication. Finally, we want to acknowledge the significant support and encouragement of colleagues in the BSA Max Weber Study Group, particularly Sam Whimster and Ralph Schroeder. We are especially grateful to Sam Whimster for numerous useful comments and references and generous assistance.

David J. Chalcraft
Austin Harrington
Mary Shields

Introduction

DAVID J. CHALCRAFT

> The obduracy with which the controversy over the 'Weber thesis' has failed to take into account Weber's *Antikritiken* is without parallel in recent scholarship.
>
> (Hennis 1988:202, note 22)

It would be foolhardy to suggest that serious attention has yet to be paid to Weber's *The Protestant Ethic and the Spirit of Capitalism*. On the contrary, this text is arguably the most famous and widely read in the classical canon of sociological writing and has been extensively debated within the discipline ever since its first appearance as a series of two articles in 1904–05. Karl Fischer, one of Weber's first critics, spoke of the 'lamentable chain of misunderstanding' as early as 1908 (Fischer 1908:38), and even though the work has been extensively studied, there is the sense that 'what Weber really meant' has only rarely been grasped. The 'academic "Thirty Years War"' which was how Lynn White characterized the Protestant Ethic (PE) debate (cited in Marshall 1982:11) has now almost become worthy of the epithet of the 'academic "Hundred Years War"'. In recent times, scholars have extended the PE debate backwards in time before 1905 and looked at the 'Weber thesis before Weber', at the cultural wars of the 1870s (Anderson 1986; Blackbourn 1988) and beyond into the wider culture where general stereotypes of 'northern Protestant energy' and 'southern Catholic indolence' were common (Münch 1993). We clearly are dealing with a thesis that confronts questions of overwhelming significance for the understanding of modernity and its rise over more than four hundred years. Less charitably, it has been argued that the reasons for the thesis' continuing fascination are 'largely a function of extraneous factors rooted deeply in the history of this century' (Piccone, 1988:97) to do with western imperialism and rationality and the West's ethnocentric

1

justification for growing social inequality (Piccone 1988:107ff.). Not many commentators, to be sure, would want to be as extreme as this, but we must not forget a long tradition of Marxist encounters with the thesis (Marshall 1982:140–57; Turner 1985).

When the literature produced by historians (e.g. Bouchard 1991; Gorski 1993; Valeri 1997; Gellner 1988; Hughes 1986, Silber 1993; Schroeder 1995, Forster 1997), theologians (Volf 1991; Badcock 1998), psychologists (Furnham 1990), and more recently by literary critics (e.g. Stachnieweski 1991; Goldman 1988, Jameson 1974; Hernes 1989; Malcolmson 1999) is added to the sociological discussions, the extent of labour expended on the essay is indeed immense. Part of the problem – in misunderstandings, disagreements and seeming 'dialogues of the deaf' – is attributable to the fact that Weber was 'bound to step on disciplinary toes' (Ray 1987:97), and many disciplines are affected by its methods and findings. It is important to keep this interdisciplinarity in mind and not to close off its interpretation from any direction, at the same time as recognising the fact that it is sociology that claims the text as classic.

In sociology itself, the PE can serve as the point of departure in the sociology of religion (see, Wilson 1982; Hamilton 1995), the sociology of development (Harrison 1988, Barnett 1988; Roberts 1995), the sociology of work (Grint 1991), sociology of organisations (Clegg 1990, Clegg 1994; du Gay 2000), and, more recently, as a significant contribution to the analysis of the cultural significance of modernity (Whimster and Lash 1987). Every year sees new contributions in various fields and it would undoubtedly take a lifetime to become fully conversant with all the literature germane to the PE. And yet, much of the history of the PE debate has been preoccupied with countering 'popular misconceptions' of Weber's thesis, through more historically and philologically based accounts. These contributions do not necessarily lead to refutations of the supposed 'real' thesis (Piccone 1988), but they certainly help to correct important misunderstandings of Weber's text. Returning to the sources may lead to the questioning of the ways in which these sub-disciplines in sociology actually do trace their origins to Weber and to the PE, and the effect of this, in turn, may be to reorient their concerns and provide new data that need to be engaged with.

Naturally, it is not possible to do justice to this debate in the short space available to me here. What I can do is highlight some key features to contextualise the first stage of the debate and the ways in which the Replies, or *Antikritiken* as they are known in German, have been received at different times. The Replies are made up of two essays responding to Karl Fischer's two reviews (Fischer 1907, 1908) and two essays responding to Rachfahl's two reviews (Rachfahl 1909, 1910). Sociology has recently entered a more historical phase in the approach to the study of the classical tradition and the decision to publish Weber's Replies to his critics reflects this concern with the quest for the historical Weber (Reisebrodt 1989). It is first necessary to outline the publication history of the Protestant Ethic thesis. After this, I turn to consider the relation of the Replies to the second version of the PE (1920), followed by a brief discussion of the first critics, Fischer and Rachfahl and historical approaches to the Weber thesis. Subsequently, a brief overview of the history of the Replies in the controversy is provided before a more detailed focus on two examples of recent work that draw on the Replies significantly. The essay concludes by offering two areas that seem ripe for further inquiry and two brief excursuses that serve to introduce elements of the intellectual and cultural context necessary to follow dimensions of Weber's Replies.

The Publication History of the Protestant Ethic Thesis

The original essays of *The Protestant Ethic and the Spirit of Capitalism* are constituted by the two articles Weber wrote in the *Archiv für Sozialwissenschaft und Sozialpolitik* in 1904 and 1905 respectively. The first article, *Die protestantische Ethik und der 'Geist' des Kapitalismus, I: Das Problem*, appeared in volume 20 of the *Archiv* in October 1904. The second article, *Die protestantische Ethik und der Geist der Kapitalismus, II: Die Berufsidee des asketischen Protestantismus*, appeared in volume 21, in June 1905. The second article was written, according to Marianne Weber (1988:356), in a three-month period of intense activity, following the Webers' return from America. Weber was in America from August to December 1904, where he had gone to deliver a lecture at the St. Louis Exhibition. On the basis of this experience, Weber also wrote his observations on the relationship between sects and capitalism, which first appeared as two brief reports in the *Frankfurter Zeitung* during April 1906 (Weber 1906a; see, Keeter 1981; Swatos 1982). These reports were subsequently rewritten and expanded, appearing in the journal, *Die christliche Welt* (Weber 1906b). In 1920 the essay on sects became better known as *Die protestantischen Sekten und der Geist des Kapitalismus*, and was the essay that followed *The Protestant Ethic* in the first volume of the *Gesammelte Aufsätze zur Religionssoziologie* ('Collected Essays in the Sociology of Religion'). This is translated as 'The Protestant Sects and the Spirit of Capitalism' in the collection edited by Gerth and Mills (Weber 1948: 302–322). The growth of the essay on sects is reflected in Weber's Replies to his critics, especially in the discussions with Rachfahl, and indeed in the second version of the PE repeated reference is made to the essay. For many commentators, Weber's arguments in the sect essay provide an important supplement to the original and revised essays (e.g. Oakes 1988, 1993).

There is ample evidence that Weber considered producing, at the suggestion of his publisher Paul Siebeck, a separate and revised version of the original essays of

1904–05 as early as 1906 (Weber 1990:119, 273, 276, 285). The issues of the *Archiv* in which it had appeared were soon sold out, and perhaps this is one of the reasons why Siebeck considered publishing a book version (Marianne Weber 1988: 326). In the Replies, Weber often complains that people are not reading his essays but rather the inaccurate reports of them by commentators such as Fischer and Rachfahl. Weber attributes this manner of reading less to their lack of availability and more to the supposed bad faith of his first readers (see pp.49 n.3, 71, 85 n.35, 95). However, Weber prevaricated and even though he mentioned in his published Reply to Fischer in 1907 that a new edition was soon to appear (see pp.34–35, 75), he seems to have become too embroiled in combating Rachfahl to have the energy or occasion to carry out the work for a new edition which (he hoped) would serve to forestall any further misunderstanding (see pp.82 n. 24, 83 n.30). Weber refers to 'personal circumstances' hindering further work on the project, (p.49 n.3), but he does not disclose these details. The frustration with lack of progress is clearly evident in the tone of the Replies and there are probably myriad reasons for the delay in working on a new edition. With the planned publication of Troeltsch's work on the social history of Protestantism, which eventually appeared in 1912, the project of a new edition was abandoned. This made economic sense to Siebeck who was also Troeltsch's publisher. At the same time, it added to Weber's frustration since Rachfahl always treated 'the thesis' as a Weber–Troeltsch partnership, and from this basis was able to create debate by highlighting the apparent differences between them.

It was not until the summer of 1919, as far as we know, that Weber returned to the idea of a second edition as part of the project to collect together his essays in the sociology of religion. Weber was living in post-war revolutionary Bavaria and his health took a turn for the worse, and it was only in his last weeks, during June 1920, that Weber conveyed his wish to dedicate to Marianne the first volume of the collected essays which were published posthumously in 1920 (Lepsius 1977; Chalcraft 1993). The three volumes of the *Gesammelte Aufsätze zur Religionssoziologie* did not contain any reprinting of Weber's Replies to his critics 1907–10.

The first volume of the *Gesammelte Aufsätze* contained: the revised version of the PE (1920:1–206); the revised version of the sects essay (1920:207–36/ 1948:302–22); a revised version of the *Einleitung* (1920:237–75/1948:267–301; based on 1915a) (English title: *The Social Psychology of the World Religions*); the revised version of the China study (1920:276–536/1951; based on 1915b), and a revised version of the essay which English readers know of as the *Intermediate Reflections* or *The Religious Rejections of the World and their Directions*, the *Zwischenbetractung* (1920:536–73/1948:323–59; based on Weber, 1915b). Weber's studies of India (1958), China (1951) and Ancient Judaism (1952), together with the *Einleitung* and *Zwischenbetractung* are collectively known as *The Economic Ethics of the World Religions* (EEWR).

The collection as a whole was prefaced with the *Vorbemerkung*, which English readers know as the *Author's Introduction*, and which was placed as the introduction to Parsons' translation of the PE in 1930. The role of the *Vorbemerkung* needs to be correctly understood, and the lack of appreciation of its late status and uneasy relation to the original versions of the PE have exercised historical critics, such as Hennis (1988) and Marshall (1982). Nelson (1974), for example, presented the *Author's Introduction* as the key to Weber's main aims. The *Vorbemerkung* was not intended, to begin with, as an introduction to the PE but to the whole series of essays on the sociology of religion. The *Vorbemerkung* certainly reflects positions Weber reached long after the original version of the PE, and one should therefore exercise considerable caution in reading the PE through its lens. In particular, the *Vorbemerkung* highlights the universal processes of rationalisation and, drawing on the comparative studies in EEWR, presents a narrative of the rise of capitalism that gives due weight to both material and ideal factors whereas the original and revised versions of the PE consciously looked at the problem from only one side of the causal chain. This particular point from the publication history is at the centre of disagreements between those seeking for a thematic unity in Weber's overall work seemingly irrespective of the biography of the work (Bendix 1960, Tenbruck 1989, Schroeder 1992, Nelson 1974) and those who ground the search for such thematic unity only in a quest for the historical Weber (Schluchter 1981, Hennis 1988). Still others consider such a search as being against a genuine historical critical interest in Weber's work (Reisebrodt 1989) and as being hermeneutically problematic (Chalcraft 1994; 2000a; 2000b). When the biography of the work is considered to be unimportant, readings of the PE tend to confuse 'PE thesis' and 'text/s', and make no references to the differences between the original and revised versions, and even when they acknowledge that key themes and concepts are absent continue to read the PE as if they were present (Schroeder 1992:96–110). Similarly, Collins' explanatory interest means that he has little truck with the quest for the historical Weber, since the PE is 'only a fragment of Weber's full theory' (Collins 1986:19). Clearly, when such interests are dominant a healthy interest in Weber's Replies to critics will not be found.

Relation of the Replies to the Second Edition of the PE

Chronologically, the Replies stand between the first and second versions of the PE and have the potential to bridge the editions and reflect, stage by stage, the growth of the PE thesis. Since the Replies only cover the years until 1910, the further development of the PE thesis takes place in other writings, namely in *The Economic Ethics of the World Religions* and in the first stages of *Economy and Society* (Schluchter 1989:411–63); but not all of these studies, of course, relate to the

PE thesis itself and looking to those texts for supplementary information on the thesis is to ignore a set of texts, the Replies, far more closely related to the problem. Such overlooking of the Replies has been the case throughout the history of the reception of the PE.

The second reason why the differences of the two editions need to be examined is that in the second version of the PE, Weber appears to be mainly concerned with the criticism of Brentano (1916) and Sombart (1915). Indeed in the revised essays Weber claims that he has not included anything from the unfruitful debates with Rachfahl. (Weber 1930: 187). Weber is being less than honest here, but knowing the heated nature of the exchanges between Weber and Rachfahl, it is not surprising to find Weber defending himself in this way. In the second Reply to Rachfahl, Weber concludes that 'after *this* critique I need not change a *single word*' (see p.77). Weber does change words and adds many new words in the second version of the PE; but what he means in both the Replies (where formulations of the original thesis are given fresh expression) and in the second version of the PE is that the great number of words he has added do not, as he sees it, change the *essential* points he has made all along. However, since Weber's hermeneutic is suspicious of any arguments that he thinks are purely concerned with semantics (see pp.66, 93, 122 n.2, 127 n.13), we ourselves must not necessarily take him 'at his word' here. To be sure, opinion varies (see, Fischoff 1944:83; note 13, Zaret 1993:245; Lehmann 1993:204; Lichtblau and Weiss 1993; Hennis 1988:27–8; Smith 1991) but it is clear that what has transpired is an empirical question which requires close analysis of the two editions, and this is now beginning to take place in earnest (Chalcraft 1992, 1994; Lichtblau and Weiss 1993); and it also requires careful thought about what constitutes a change and where meaning resides.

A close analysis of the two editions reveals that at least the following points are significant. Passages that present the 'disenchantment of the world' thesis are new to the second version (1930:109, 117). The role of psychological sanctions is more greatly stressed in the second (e.g. 1930:197). There is an increased discussion of the issue of tolerance and its relation to the problems at hand (1930:242ff.). The distinction between Catholic and Calvinist theologies of absolution is made more of (1930:106). The presentation of Franklin is greatly qualified (1930:51ff.). The linguistic discussion of forms of the calling is significantly extended (1930: 204 ff.; see, Hanyu, 1994; Chalcraft 1992: 234–80). Weber discusses at length the ethos that animated Alberti (1930:194–8) in direct response to Sombart (1915). The quotation from Wesley and the reference to processes of the secularising of wealth do not appear in the original essays (1930:175). There is detailed discussion of the closer linking of monasticism and Protestant asceticism and of life and attitudes to economy in the Middle Ages in general. The firmer distinction between the modern spirit of capitalism and all forms of devotion to money and its acquisition occasions many alterations (1930:52, 57f.). The bringing in of 'contemporary witnesses' to secure the proverbial status of the relation between piety and business sense runs like a *leitmotiv* through the second version (1930:43), as does the elaboration of distinctions between past and present and the continuing legacies from the past (1930:37). References to the sects essay and Troeltsch's work are now possible; and there is increased empirical reference to the Dutch case and to events in North America. To this far from complete list needs to be added myriad numbers of additions, replacements and omissions that affect the sense but which cannot be easily summarized. Being aware of some of the items that change and develop alerts the commentator to their absence and presence in the Replies and it becomes harder to support Weber's claim that nothing is carried forward from them. For example, references to Sir William Petty (1930:179), private fortunes in Hamburg (1930: 191), ways of life in the Wuppertal (1930:44) and the example of Sebastian Franck (1930:121) are all new features in the second version that can arguably be traced to the exchanges with Rachfahl.

The First Critics of the Replies and Historical
Approaches to the Weber Thesis

Full bibliographical details and summaries of the argument of the essays by Fischer and Rachfahl are given at the start of each Reply (see chapters 1, 3, 5 and 7). At the present time, little is known of H. Karl Fischer and we have not succeeded in identifying him. There were a number of Fischers active in academic, literary and professional life whose forenames render them just about eligible, but none have been discovered in the records who fit conclusively. The strongest candidate is probably Dr Karl Fischer (born 1840) of Wiesbaden, who published a large number of works from 1870 onwards on German history, including medieval history and culture, with a marked interest in pedagogy but ranging also over politics, economics, philosophy, psychology and religious belief, although from 1901 he seems to have written mainly on the poet Eduard Mörike. Other candidates seem less likely.

More is known of Professor Felix Rachfahl (1867–1925). He was a historian who wrote extensively on Dutch and German history. His most important work was a three-volume history of William of Orange and the sixteenth to seventeenth century Dutch revolt against Spain (published 1906, 1907–8 and 1924). He lectured at the universities of Kiel, Halle, Königsberg and Giessen before returning to Kiel in 1909, the year he published his first critique of Weber. His last move was to Freiburg in 1914, where he was vice-chancellor in 1922–23, and died in post. In most of these posts he taught modern history, but in Königsberg (1903–07) medieval history; and in his medieval research he concentrated particularly on economic and constitutional questions. His autobiography was published in a collection of autobiographies of contemporary historians from 1926 entitled *Geschichtswissenschaft der Gegenwart in Selbstdarstellungen* (Prades 1969:89; see, Davis 1978).

Both Fischer and Rachfahl were historians, albeit of different stripes, and both approached Weber with this interpretative interest uppermost. The marriage between history and sociology has not always been a happy one and in the case of the PE debate there have been long periods of separation which have led to divorce in some instances (Pellicani 1988). Yet it is impossible to deny that the PE has an explanatory empirical dimension. However much one may point out that Weber's chosen task was not to establish a strict causal empirical relation between business and piety but to provide an *interpretation* of that relation (see, Winckelmann 1978:8), and however much one accepts that the thesis is based on probabilities and affinities rather than definite casual chains, and, again, however much one emphasises its great imaginative and empathic insight into the harrowing psychological life of Calvinists and sectarians – at some point episte-mological and evidential questions have to be faced. And this means that the work of historians and historical sociologists is essential. Sociology, in the last analysis, is an empirical discipline and along with history needs to weigh factual evidence and causal accounts.

The difficulty with accepting the findings of historians is less that some are in support of Weber's thesis while others are not (Oakes 1988) but the suspicion that they may be working with completely different conceptions of ideal types, capitalism, spirit of capitalism and ascetic Protestantism, so that their terms do not relate to Weber's and they report on different phenomena, making dialogue diffi-cult. It is essential for the refutation of the thesis, and advances in scholarship, for the account to be tested in ways that are relevant to its actual claims and purposes (Marshall 1980, 1982, Oakes 1993, Tyrell 1990). These were precisely the episte-mological points Weber made to his first critics. In the Replies, Weber provides further discussion of empirical cases and demarcates what types of evidence are significant and which are not, in particular discussing at length aspects of North American and Dutch history relevant to the case.

It is on similar grounds of relevance to Weber's original essays and the Replies that I do not discuss below those works of psychologists (e.g. Furnham 1990) and sociologists (Bouma 1973/91; Jones 1997) that seek to operationalise and test variables and models generated from the PE in contemporary settings. Simi-larly, work in the sociology of development that rests on the premise that the EEWR series is the planned negative testing of the positive correlation between religious values and economic life presented in the PE cannot be evaluated here (Swatos 1998).

The History of the Replies in the PE Debate: A Brief Overview

The first stage of the debate from 1907–10 took on the colour that it did not only because of what was said but also because of the manner in which it was conducted. The style of the exchanges between Fischer and Weber, and even more so between Rachfahl and Weber, is just as significant as the fact that there were central disagreements over a range of factual and epistemological issues. These latter included (see, Davis 1978:1106–08; Samuelson 1961:8–11; Ray 1987; Fischoff 1944): the exact intentions Weber had in mind; the definitions of the spirit of capitalism and how this ethos was distinctive compared to previous approaches to money and business; the way the latter distinction was confused in the case of the contrast of Franklin and Fugger; the definition and meaning of inner-worldly asceticism and whether it was meaningful to use such a label given the meaning of asceticism in Catholic monasticism and everyday speech; the argument that for Luther to have used the concept of calling in the specific sense meant by Weber it would have had to have been already familiar to ordinary people and hence built on prior material changes in society; the method Weber adopted and the emphasis given to ideal and material factors; the possibility of the admission of insights from psychology; the interpretation of the significance of tolerance and the growth of the spirit of capitalism in particular European cities and states; the question of what Weber wanted to write about next but was unable to undertake; the interpretation of the evidence concerning early economic growth in North America, the influence of Calvinism in Holland and the role of the rising middle classes in England and the decline of Merrie Old England. There was also acrimonious discussion of the relation between Weber and Troeltsch's work, against both of whom Rachfahl's 1909 essay was addressed. Troeltsch replied in the same journal in which Rachfahl's review appeared (the *Internationale Wochenschrift*), but Weber felt himself 'dishonoured' by the fact that the editors of this journal had only approached Troeltsch for a response, not himself (see p.61). It is at this point that it is impossible to separate the content from the style and language of the debate (Chalcraft 2001c).

Rachfahl and Weber both accuse each other of willful misreading, childishness, disciplinary patriotism (*Ressortspatriotismus*), cliquishism, incompetence (stepping outside of the established boundaries of academic discussion, governed as they were by strict rules of remit, like state departments); ignorance; dishonour; utilising strategies more suited to low-level politics, street theatre and magic shows; pedantry, hair-splitting bookishness, 'Talmudism' (see p.122 n.2) and immature fixation on words and particular sentences.

That Weber's Replies have not been studied in depth, given the strength and longevity of interest in the PE debate, is almost beyond comprehension. It is surely important not to reinvent continually the wheel of criticism, but it is even more important to consider carefully what Weber wrote in return and to consider carefully what we learn about Weber's argument (van Duelman 1988:77; Davis 1978), context and person in the process (Roth 1992, 1993). The PE debate certainly 'has not gone off the boil' as the exchanges, for example, between Cohen (1980, 1983) and Holton (1983), Oakes and Pellicani in 1988 and the response to Mackinnon (1988, 1993) by many scholars (e.g. Zaret 1993, Oakes 1993) indicate. It is clear that the debate cannot be effectively carried out, or progressed, without the full textual evidence being considered, and this means that *all* the texts need to be made readily available, and not only to a specialised audience but to all practitioners in social science, many of whom are readers of English. As Sica observes, 'without complete, reliable translations, scholarship is forever strapped by various levels of inadequacy, if not outright inaccuracy' (Sica 1984:16). The present translation of Weber's Replies to his critics seeks to redress these textual lacunae, and such work would have met with the approval of scholars such as Fischoff (1944:16), Davis (1978) and Marshall (1982:14).

The Replies in More Recent Debate: Two Examples

1 The debate between Pellicani and Oakes

The Replies have played a more significant role in more recent debates such as that between Pellicani (1988, 1989) and Oakes (1988, 1989, 1993). After a survey of historical literature, Pellicani reaches the strong conclusion that: 'The PE is of no help in resolving the mystery of the birth of capitalism, nor does it contribute to even identifying factors which stimulated the development of the entrepreneurial spirit' (1988:84). The hypothesis, he continues, is 'in conflict with everything that historiography has ascertained concerning the nature of Calvinism and its long term consequences' (1988:85). It is 'a work which should be put aside once and for all' (1988:85).

Oakes replies by pointing out that Weber's position has been incorrectly presented. Pellicani's opinion of the Replies is that while they are 'indispensable for a reconstruction of the debate', they 'contain nothing new' (1989:63; note 2). Oakes, on the other hand, stresses 'the contribution these responses make to the clarification of the main problem of *The Protestant Ethic* and a more precise statement of its principal thesis, matters that are framed only informally, and frequently metaphorically, in the 1904–5 essays' (1989:91; note 17). 'Here Weber clarifies the intention and the problematic that underpin his two original essays and also disposes of various errors he ascribes to his critics' (Oakes 1988:82). Pellicani offers a different thesis of the rise of capitalism from Weber. For Pellicani, it is institutional and political change that is essential for the growth of capitalism, namely 'the weakening of hierocratic institutions animated solely by fear of mammon' (1989:73). Oakes outlines at least four dimensions of the exchanges with Fischer and Rachfahl that should have forestalled some of Pellicani's errors.

2 Wilhelm Hennis and the significance of Weber's Replies to Fischer and Rachfahl

For Hennis, the Replies clear up major misunderstandings not only about the PE thesis, but also about Weber's 'central question', and are the key to the thematic unity of Weber's work. 'It is for this reason', Hennis writes, 'that these writings should in fact have been regarded for the past 75 years as the most important supplementary texts on the Weber "thesis"!' (Hennis 1988:28).

Hennis challenges many assumptions within the sociological reception of Weber's work, and his inquiry is motivated by a desire to uncover 'which leading question and intention might lie at the foundation of the work as a whole' (1988:22) and to move away from fragmentary and reductive readings. This requires reading Weber 'afresh' and 'without prejudice', and this means the entire corpus of his work (1988:22). Tenbruck's suggestion (1975/89) that the central question was the theme of rationalisation processes and disenchantment cannot hold, Hennis argues, since the theme has 'no relevance for an analysis of the Protestant Ethic' (1988:23). The way to uncover the central question is to look at the controversies of the day and how Weber responded to them. In this light, Weber's responses to Fischer and Rachfahl are unique and highly significant to the task at hand since Weber was forced to articulate what his key question was. This is especially possible because we have two versions of the PE that allow us to compare and contrast Weber's positions over a 15–year period. A closing sentence in the PE, which remains unchanged in the second version, provides a key. The sentence runs: '*One of the fundamental elements* of the spirit of modern capitalism, and not only of that but *of all modern culture: rational conduct* on the basis of the idea of the calling, *was born* – that is what this discussion has sought to demonstrate – *out of the spirit of Christian asceticism*' (Weber 1930:180; (Hennis's italics)). With these emphases, 'we can conclude', Hennis adds, that the 'theme of 1905, just like that of 1920, would be the genealogy of the modern "rational *Lebensführung*" ['rational conduct of life'] by a "historical representation"'. In the text of 1920, Weber found 'nothing on which he could improve', apart from 'a tiny editorial insertion' (1988:27). Further, the outlining of the research programme at the close of the PE is nothing less than the consideration of those other aspects not captured in the 'one fundamental element' above: such pointers are clear from the interchange with Rachfahl. Hennis then draws the conclusion. Weber's 'theme is thus not some process of rationalization "in general", but rather that of the process of rationalization of "practical *Lebensführung*"' (1988: 45). To be precise, it is not the rationalisation of practical *Lebensführung* in general that concerns Weber but the impact of rationalisation on the specific conduct of life of those humans caught in the iron cage of modernity. This central question can also be found articulated in other works that are perhaps less-well known but in which Weber had to be clear about the central question he was addressing. This central question about the fate of humanity in a variety of social orders serves to place Weber in an ancient tradition of cultural and political inquiry, a tradition that cannot be captured if Weber is turned into a narrow founding father of sociology (Thomas 1998).

Yet it is sociology, one could rejoin, that appreciates Weber as 'the foremost social theorist of modernity' (Whimster and Lash 1987:1). Returning to consider the Replies, with some of Hennis's points in mind, together with the sociological interest in modernity, there is much of importance relating to Weber's analysis of the fate of humanity in the 'iron cage of modernity' from the original and revised essays of the PE. For example, the unified Puritan personality, which managed to achieve a unique balancing of the 'great inner tensions and conflicts between calling, ethos and life' (see p.73, cf. 102–3), is to be contrasted, Weber emphasises, with the human beings of the Middle Ages who had no need to seek such a unity – unless, that is, they were major economic actors on the model of the Renaissance trader – and with contemporary individuals who experience disunity as a major cultural problem. Rachfahl does not agree with this analysis of the 'torn' (*zerrissene*) personality. For Weber, modern persons are trapped within the 'gears' and 'machinery' (*Getriebe*) of modern capitalism. This is not quite an 'iron cage' (Chalcraft, 1994; Scott, 1997): in two passages in the Replies (see pp.117, 130 n.20) Weber speaks of the *Getriebe* in which people are entangled against their will, translated here by 'hurly-burly' to suggest the whir of the machines and the blur of the mechanical noise that deafens the people with vocations and confuses and frightens away those sensitive humanistic, artistic and poetic natures that retreat from capitalism. Puritanism provided the 'corresponding soul' for the objective needs and forms of modern capitalism in its early stages (see pp.73, 130 n.20), and the question therefore arises as to whether there will be a corresponding soul that is perfectly suited to today's demands and style of life but still capable of authentic moral existence. These are the questions of value, of judgement and faith that Weber does not explore further at the close of the PE, and he does not explore them further here, but it is fair to say that the urgency of the issue that can be felt in Hennis' reconstruction of the central question finds more than an echo in the Replies.

Further Research and Two Excursuses on the Academic and Cultural Context of the Replies

Below, I offer two areas for further research, and two interpretative sections that serve to illuminate linguistic and cultural aspects of the Replies that require introductory comment. These are, first, Fischer's and Weber's understanding of 'reflective psychology' (*Reflexionspsychologie*) and, second, the language of the *Mensur*: the student fencing fraternities that provide a context for the attitudes to honour in public and private life that are encountered in the debate with Rachfahl (see, Ay 1998).

Literary and linguistic concerns

For those with a literary–linguistic interpretative interest, the Replies are quite fascinating. Since they are data to be interpreted and provide further knowledge of Weber's lexicon and modes of expression, they present many avenues for further research. The Replies contain allusions and direct references to literary works, including Shakespeare and Baudelaire (see pp.78 n.12, 80 n.14). It is perhaps not coincidental, given the concerns of Baudelaire and the symbolist poets with whom Weber was acquainted, such as Maeterlinck, that in the PE and the Replies a constant source for metaphors of social change and social relations are Dutch coastal and inland landscapes – dykes, dams, polders, waterways and canals – and that the way in which conceptions of 'affinity' are expressed in the Replies is by means of 'correspondence' and 'soul'. Beyond these interests, it would also be instructive to investigate Weber's pools of meaning, especially his constructions of strings of insults and his punning, as well as his uses of language from legal, military, psychoanalytic and popular journalistic settings. All of these dimensions are worthy of further analysis and should tell us much about Weber's linguistic universe (essential for progression in translation issues) as well as his knowledge of, and relation to, literary and artistic movements such as symbolism and expressionism (see Chalcraft 1993; 1998; 2000a; 2000c; 2001b; Shields 1998).

Further research: misunderstanding and Weber's textual hermeneutics

Since the PE debate has so often been labelled as one of 'misunderstanding', and given that the point of departure for any understanding is Weber's own communications in written form, it is clear that issues of hermeneutics and interpretation should play a central role. Weber's own approach to reading, paraphrase, quotation and meaning is equally significant and we can witness his approach directly in the Replies. Suffice to say here that it appears that Weber's hermeneutics was somewhat compromised by social and personal relations. For example, Weber allows his colleagues – Troeltsch, for example, or Sombart (see, Lehmann 1993), to have different purposes when investigating the same areas, and he permits them the right of paraphrase and occasional inaccuracy, and even terminological differences. This courtesy is not extended to Rachfahl, even when he is deserving (which is not always). Further, Weber, at times, hardly holds to a consistent distinction between public and private realms of argument or evidence and this causes him, and his critics, difficulties since they become unsure as to the status of anecdotal and personal evidence and as to when this evidence is admissible. A particular case is the running debate over the meaning of asceticism and the consumption of oysters that occupies Weber and Rachfahl (see, Chalcraft 2001a).

If one is to wring the last drop of meaning from textual evidence, for Weber that is going too far. Fixating on particular words is also objectionable. On the other hand, he expects precision in terminological instances, but finds debate about his terminology to be sterile. Terminology is to be derived from general linguistic usage, but when confronted with an argument concerning that general usage, scholars' right to define their own concepts is invoked. Further, he expects to be correctly reported and not strangely paraphrased, but when Rachfahl accuses him of misquoting others and highlights particular words that he has indeed misquoted, he considers this hair-splitting. Yet, when discussing the meaning of a Franklin or a Luther or a Sir William Petty, it is the case that what they said in particular places and contexts *in their texts* is at the heart of the matter and Weber is willing to discuss this interpretation on the basis of text. One searches in vain for a consistent hermeneutic for Weber *in these exchanges*.

Intellectual and cultural context: Karl Fischer and the value of historical psychology

At the heart of Fischer's debate with Weber is a discussion about the value of 'reflective psychology' (*Reflexionspsychologie*) for historical work and this needs some introduction. Fischer concludes that given what he sees as Weber's one-sided idealist account of the rise of capitalism and Sombart's one-sided materialist account, the debate about the origins of capitalism has reached an impasse and his contribution is to provide a psychological explanation to account for the historical problems raised. An approach based in psychology, he argues, would demonstrate that the spirit cannot be derived from Puritanism and that much of what Weber describes can be seen as psychological developments accommodating to already existing material conditions.

The ahistorical nature of the conceptions used by Fischer, such as 'the pleasure of the individual in active exertion' or the grouping together of what to Weber are persons with 'a quite heterogeneous range of mentalities' (see p.36), means, Weber argues, that essential differences are not grasped, and the singularity of the devotion to the calling in ascetic Protestantism cannot be grasped through such imprecision – certainly not when facts are made to follow theories and forced onto Procrustean beds of *a priori* psychological categories. Indeed, what cannot emerge in such deductive reasoning is any appreciation of the world-views and the sincere beliefs held by the subjects under discussion and the way in which 'our forebears' considered religious ideas about salvation and the afterlife to be fundamental (p.36; see 1930:104, 183). Fischer works with out-moded and spurious-looking conceptions of 'the autonomously determined concept of duty' and the 'heteronomously determined concept of duty' (Fischer 1907:22) that Weber does right to ignore.

Turning to Ficher's second review and Weber's second Reply, we find that Fischer (1908), for his part, feels that Weber has missed 'the crux of the question'. The crux of the question for Fischer seems to move from his preoccupation with materialism and idealism in his first review towards a greater focus on the methodological issue of the psychological assumptions imported into the account by Weber. The latter issue, however, is linked to the former since the psychology that Fischer defends clearly shows to him that the origin of the calling and the valuing of money as an end in itself can only be a reflection of, and adaptation to, already existing economic practices and ideas. For Weber, the crux of the question in this regard is that understanding of the psychological motives of historical individuals can only be based on knowledge of the sources. For Fischer, however, to look for 'methodical conduct of life' involves researchers in using 'reflective psychology' whether they like it or not.

Fischer also speaks of 'reflective psychology' in his first review and it appears to have a status as a specific approach within the discipline. It is the case that a reflective psychology was founded at Würzburg by Oswald Külpe where he was professor 1894–1909, and further championed by Karl Bühler (1879–1963) but it seems far more likely that Fischer is using this term very loosely and merely means retrojection of one's own psychic states or motivations, based on amateur self-reflection and observation. Clearly, Fischer would not be as castigating of 'exact' introspection, as carried out experimentally by Wilhelm Wundt (1832–1920), as a basis for scientific knowledge (see, Miller 1962:25–39). Indeed, Fischer twice cites the work of Gustav Wilhelm Stoerring, a pupil of Wundt's, at this time professor in Zurich (1902–11). However, even Wundtian psychological practice, in Weber's view, leads to overly complicated formulations. Weber himself was in no doubt about the exiguous value of Wundt's psychology for historical research, including both Wundt's methodology of 'introspection through apperception' and the *Völkerpsychologie* for which he is famous. For example, in *Roscher and Knies*, Weber argues that despite Wundt's 'comprehensive intellectual achievement', Wundt's conceptions are value-laden and smack of positivist conceptions of norms and laws that could only inhibit historical objectivity, which must be based on empirical study and actual causality (Weber 1905a:111, 128; see, Frommer and Frommer 1990; Harrington 2000:449.).

There is certainly a lot that is hard to make sense of in Fischer's proposals here. Fischer ends by doubting whether Weber recognises that 'our very knowledge and assessment of historical objects is not possible without certain – I am sorry to say – *psychological* presuppositions' (Fischer 1908:43). Weber's response to this makes use of a wicked humour in which psycho-speak is utilised to parody Fischer's postures (see Chalcraft 2001c). He replies by saying that 'history – "I am sorry to say" – makes "general psychological assumptions" *only* in the sense that it makes general "astronomical assumptions"' (see p.48).

The language and culture of the Mensur in Weber's exchanges with Rachfahl

It is Rachfahl himself who uses the language of the duelling fraternities (McAleer 1994) for the first time, and Weber responds directly. For sure, it is Weber that has spoken of disloyalty and dishonour, and it is Weber that has trafficked in personal insults, but it is Rachfahl who soberly wonders how far this can all go. 'Was Weber', he asks at one point, 'actually aware of the gravity of this reproach?' (Rachfahl 1910:219).

Rachfahl, in speaking of Troeltsch's misquoting, uses the analogy of duelling to question Troeltsch's method: 'Thus he constructs a phantom for himself, passes it off as his opponent's opinion, and valiantly hits out at it. A polemic of this nature is condemned to sterility' (Rachfahl 1910:234). Such a strike in a duel scores no points. Rachfahl uses similar language for Weber, when he too is seen as inventing statements and attributing them to Rachfahl. 'That is once again the tried-and-tested fencing move: to set up a bogey, present it as the opponent's opinion, and boldly take a lunge at it' (*Das ist wieder einmal das bewährte Fechterstückchen, – einen Popanz herzustellen, als Meinung des Gegners auszugeben und wacker drauf los zu pauken*) (Rachfahl, 1910:245). At times, the person of the opponent is mentioned in disparaging ways, pointing not only to his academic incompetence but also calling his masculinity in doubt. Rachfahl opines that 'such a way of doing combat' proves nothing except the 'inner weakness of the person who uses it' (Rachfahl 1910:264). For Rachfahl, Weber is rash, quick to anger, and a person whose judgements, both personal and academic, must be questioned. He writes that Weber's style of attack 'betrays an excitability that has destroyed all perceptiveness and proper judgement' (Rachfahl 1910:249).

For his part, Weber replies to this explicit language of the *Mensur* by speaking of 'swine strokes' ('as we used to call them in the student argot') and 'strokes below the belt' (see p.121 n.1). He continues: 'This duelling pleasure of his typically becomes so rampant and unbridled as to constantly fall short of its "object"'. Yet throughout, Weber deflects the full force of the duel by turning Rachfahl into an unworthy opponent and presenting him as a clumsy novice. Weber questions the maturity of his opponent even to enter the fray when he says that 'in any other writer with thicker blood in his veins, I would have to call this an impertinence; but since Rachfahl sees little harm in such practices, I may as well spare myself the effort' (see p.125). Weber is responding directly to the accusation that he has not read a particular authority on Dutch history, but does not pursue satisfaction for the impertinence and only questions Rachfahl's intent.

Related to the *Mensur* are a range of related insults and sarcastic phrases that appear to draw on the language of the student argot as well as the vista of the cheaper sides of American politics where Weber was undoubtedly drawing on his own experiences from the 1904 visit to the United States. The key words here are forms of *'Klopffechter'*. *'Fechter'* relates to fencing and hence to duelling. The element *'Klopf'*, refers to banging, clanging and knocking. The compound noun *'Klopffechter'* then extends to the meaning of 'hand-to-hand fighting' or with instruments that 'knock and clang' when struck together. It is also a figurative term for argument, for rowdy argument and controversialism. In the *Mensur* setting, one can see how *'Klopffechter'* would refer to a particularly bad swordsman, noisy, clumsy, undisciplined, making many wild and dangerous strokes. In the context of public debate and politics especially, a *'Klopffechter'* would be a rowdy, polemical, hollow rhetorician, inciting the crowd by manipulation.

The translation preferred in the present text is 'wrangler' (pp.120, 121 n.1), chosen not least because it is hardly possible to convey all the meanings above with one choice word. 'Wrangler' (and 'wrangling') is preferred since this nicely conjures up the notions of argument, often for the sake of being argumentative, but also of wrestling and fighting (see p.128–29). In America, a 'wrangler' evokes the American cowboy wrestling with the cattle to brand them, or fencing off great plains to keep the cattle from straying too far (see the next paragraph, on 'nailing down'). The tricks (pp.96–97) and 'sleights of hand' (p.124 n.8 – *Klopffechterkunstgriff*) encountered in the second Reply to Rachfahl are linked with some of the imagery in previous Replies about charlatan card tricks (see p.49: 'rustling up phrases' or 'shaking sentences out of one's sleeve' ['*Sätze aus dem Armel … zu schütteln*']) and 'rabbits out of hats' – 'conjuring up' economic conditions (p.34) – that serve to convey that Fischer's and Rachfahl's arguments are as bad and unconvincing as the techniques in bad operas and poor dramas where events come 'out of the blue' (p.104) or the denouement is conveyed by 'spirits rising from the grave' (p.97). But the *Klopffechterkunstgriff* can now be seen to also include clumsy attempts to carry off particular strokes, thrusts and parries, in a duelling situation or as tricky and deft dodges that border on the illegal. The latter sense is found (see p.104) where 'cack-handed' seemed the most appropriate rendering.

All of these ideas are associated with Weber's playing with language for the effect of rendering his opponent, his debater, shamed and incompetent. When Rachfahl reckons to have 'nailed' Weber down, Weber can play with this notion in both senses of wrangler. To pin an argument down, to specify precisely what is at issue and where someone has indeed been false or misleading such that he now openly confesses it, is associated with the notions of a wrestler pinning their opponent down in a swift and effective move. Weber accuses Rachfahl of emitting a triumphant cry – 'a how's that?' – just as Rachfahl in turn accuses Weber of doing the same, appealing to the umpire that a strike on the person has been accomplished by this good argument.

For Rachfahl, the nailing down of Weber is to indicate where meaning resides to Weber's own discredit. For Weber, Rachfahl's desire to nail him down is but another example of his wrangling as an argumentative pugilist turned into physical wrestler. How such a clumsy, grubby-handed duellist can ever hope to score a hit, can ever entertain the notion that he has pinned down and defeated someone as sophisticated as himself, Weber cannot begin to countenance. How else can Rachfahl score victories other than by lying in wait to ambush him down one of the nooks and crannies ('*Schlupfwinkel*', p.93) of the 'Talmudic' (p.122) debate he leads his unsuspecting victim into? Using Rachfahl's own phrasing – and not for the first time – Weber turns the tables on him. There is no doubt in Weber's mind: Rachfahl is 'a part-time, dilettante, meddling wrangler' (pp.131–32) who should keep his envenomed foil sheathed and watch from the sidelines.

For Weber, the nailing down of Rachfahl is to expose his childish and amateur critique.

> So, leaving aside the obvious answer to what has been 'nailed down' here, let *me* now 'nail down' Rachfahl's question: what spirit can have bred a 'review' that sees its business in *nothing more* than trying to 'nail down' the author to individual *words* and *sentences* – and moreover constantly failing ? From A to Z, you will find nothing but this in Rachfahl's 'review' and 'reply'.
>
> (p.129)

Final Comment

In the history of reception to date, for many of the reasons outlined above, to do with the non-availability of translations, Weber's own dismissive comments, and dominant interpretative interests in sociology, the ideas of the first critics and more importantly Weber's Replies to them have not met with the degree of attention they deserve. The work of Oakes and Hennis provide good examples of the types of scholarly advances that can be made when they are given serious attention, but it is clear that their work far from exhausts their significance for us (see Roth 1992, 1993). I have outlined above some areas for further research and provided some detail concerning two intellectual and cultural–linguistic contexts to aid understanding of particular features of the Replies. There is much more that could be said.

The essays are significant: not only in the quest for the historical Weber and for accuracy in the mapping of the history of the Protestant Ethic debate and for grasping Weber's developing projects and his *Wissenschaftslehre* but also in our attempts to develop a contemporary Weberian sociology that seriously addresses the cultural and social issues of our day.

Translators' Note

Talcott Parsons' translation of *The Protestant Ethic* from 1930 has been enormously influential in the reception of Weber's work in the English-speaking world. Today, however, most scholars accept that Parsons' translation is seriously defective. Parsons' text suffers from numerous inaccuracies and an excessive use of paraphrase that neglects the unique nuances of the original and tends to want to stretch Weber's writing onto the Procrustean bed of Parsons' own quite distinct vision of sociology. It also generally emasculates Weber's richly metaphorical vocabulary, substituting anodyne or truncated words like 'practical ethics' for *Berufsethik*, 'life' for *Lebensstil*, 'suitable' for *adäquat*, 'religion' for *Religiosität* and 'correlation' or 'intimate relationship' instead of 'affinity' or 'elective affinity' for *Verwandschaft* and *Wahlverwandschaft* (see Ghosh 1994). The later translations of the methodological writings by Shils and Finch (Weber 1949) and the now classic collection of Gerth and Wright Mills (Weber 1948) certainly improve on Parsons, although it has been felt that even they still suffer from too much doctoring of vocabulary, especially in the case of the methodological writings, which have been accused of obscuring the specific Neo-Kantian context of Weber's reflections (Hinkle 1986; Hennis 1988). Only over the last two or three decades, with the gradual emancipation of sociological studies from the positivist residues that still dogged sociology in the early to mid-twentieth century, have commentators come to respect the unique literary qualities of the sociological classics. Scholars today expect a much higher standard of attention to the technical constructions, neologisms and other idiosyncrasies of an author than was the case fifty years ago and are much more willing to tolerate alien vocabulary for the sake of accuracy. This is the spirit in which the present translation has been written.

Our translation seeks to reflect the distinct style of Weber's lexicon as faithfully as possible. We make a point of preserving his copious and rather excessive inverted commas, italicised emphases and lengthy paragraphs, and we try to find English equivalents for keywords and neologisms that mirror the German as closely as possible. On the other hand, we have not followed these maxims absolutely. The original German is somewhat turgid, certainly not among Weber's most elegant pieces of writing; and this probably goes some way to explaining why the Replies have not been translated until now. The sentences are generally extremely long, often containing up to five or six different sub-clauses and parentheses with frequent intensifiers such as *eben*, *ja* and *gewiß* and other pleonastic expressions, as well as a ubiquitous use of the superlative. A translation that sought to preserve all these features would have been completely unreadable. It is quite likely that Weber dashed off these Replies at speed, without reworking or refining the text subsequently. Certainly the rambling and convoluted syntax gives a strong sense of the desire to build up walls of fortification around himself, to build an impregnable discursive fortress clearly explicable in terms of the underlying tone of indignation that runs throughout. We have therefore decided to break down Weber's Teutonic sentences into smaller units and to use syntax always in a way that is natural and feasible in English. Sometimes we have added extra paragraph breaks and omitted italics where they distort or clutter the semantic focus of the sentence or where there is no corresponding word in the English text. (It should be noted that Wallace Davis also makes modifications of this nature in his own admirable translation of the final Section II of the fourth Reply from 1978 (Weber 1978a). Our translation makes no claim to improve on Davis's version of this section, although it does follow Weber's phrase constructions slightly more directly.)

To be true to an author, one must also, in a sense, be untrue. Translators want to convey the unique qualities of the original, and yet they have no option but to draw as expressively as possible on the resources of their own language. As Walter Benjamin (1970) once emphasised, all translations are new creations in their own right, new accretions in the infinite embroidery of signification, never simple reproductions of their 'objects'. A translation arguably does most justice to the original when it allows the author to speak eloquently to us in the idioms of our own language.

In this translation of the Replies, references to the original essay are to the *Archiv* version of 1904–05 and to the English translation of the revised version of 1920 by Talcott Parsons. *Archiv* volume numbers are denoted by Roman numerals, with page numbers after the colon (eg. XX:26). Parsons' page numbers follow *Archiv* references after the stroke (/) and are denoted by 'PE' (eg. XX:26/PE:64). Note that in the editors' footnotes to this text, not all the quotations from Parsons' translation correspond exactly to the first edition of the essay since no English translation exists of the original *Archiv* version.

The present translation follows Johannes Winckelmann's edition of the Replies (1978). Winckelmann's editing consists mainly of standardising the *Archiv* references (Weber sometimes uses the equivalent of loc. cit., sometimes not, and sometimes puts references in brackets, sometimes not) and standardising orthography. In the second Reply to Rachfahl, Winckelmann makes some small omissions where the text becomes especially vituperative. These have been replaced with the original *Archiv* text. Winckelmann's edition also contains the full text of the reviews of Weber's essay by Karl Fischer and Felix Rachfahl, and all references to Fischer's and Rachfahl's reviews here are to Winckelmann's page numbers. The *Archiv* sources of Weber's Replies are as follows:

- First Reply to Fischer: 'Kritische Bemerkungen zu den vorstehenden "Kritischen Beiträgen"', *Archiv für Sozialwissenschaft und Sozialpolitik*, vol. XXV, 1907, pp.243–49.
- Second Reply to Fischer: 'Bemerkungen zu der vorstehenden "Replik"', *Archiv für Sozialwissenschaft und Sozialpolitik*, vol. XXVI, 1908, pp.275–83.
- First Reply to Rachfahl: 'Antikritisches zum "Geist" des Kapitalismus', *Archiv für Sozialwissenschaft und Sozialpolitik*, vol. XXX, 1910, pp.176–202.
- Second Reply to Rachfahl: 'Antikritisches Schlußwort zum "Geist des Kapitalismus"', *Archiv für Sozialwissenschaft und Sozialpolitik*, vol. XXXI, 1910, pp.554–99.

Austin Harrington

Part I

CHAPTER 1

Karl Fischer's Review of
The Protestant Ethic, 1907

From the *Archiv für Sozialwissenschaft und Sozialpolitik*, vol. 25, pp. 232–42

Summary

Fischer's central strategy is to dispute what he sees as Weber's 'idealist interpretation of history'. He considers some alternative material and economic factors for the spread of capitalism in early modern Europe, and concludes with what he claims is a more plausible 'psychological' explanation for the rise of capitalist mentalities. In general, his position is that while the correlation between confessional affiliation and capitalist development may be in some countries remarkable, it does not permit us actually to 'derive' (*ableiten*) the spirit of capitalism from Puritanism.

Fischer begins by arguing that in his translation of the relevant passages in the Bible, Luther could not have thought of using the German word *Beruf*, with the sense of 'worldly calling', unless this sense of the word already existed for ordinary people. The religious sense of duty in one's worldly vocation cannot have been entirely Luther's innovation; it must have already been familiar to the people:

> Even assuming ... Luther achieved something original here, this is still not necessarily proof that his religious ideas generated the concept of the calling. For how did Luther arrive at the idea of using *Beruf* for his translation of the passage in Jesus Sirach? Presumably, he could not have meant his Bible translation to create a religious system in which even work in a worldly calling was to have a place. Rather, he must have thought that by using this common expression, he was choosing the best, most easily understandable term for ordinary people. Thus the 'spirit' of Luther's Bible translation may simply have been adapted to common discourse.
>
> (1907:13)

Fischer therefore suggests that the religious aspect of worldly callings could equally well be explained in terms of adaptation to already existent economic circumstances. He considers why the 'signs of election' so central to Puritanism should have been sought precisely in work in a calling, rather than in any other activity or state of being. For the Puritans to think in terms of relationships of debt to God, key economic institutions must have already been in place. Similarly, he questions the significance Weber ascribes to Baptist communities for capitalist activity, objecting that the early radical Baptist practice of withdrawing from all unnecessary contact with worldly people and intensely 'waiting' for the descent of the Holy Spirit could not easily have lent itself to sober penny-counting. Moreover, the later return of Baptist communities to normal society could only have occurred as a result of growing economic imperatives, not due to some inner 'logic of development' in a crypto-Hegelian sense.

In support of his alternative materialist account, Fischer cites Werner Sombart's analysis of the growing demand for money in the Middle Ages after the return of the crusaders (Sombart 1902). Where monarchies gained money by imposing new taxes and the nobility through sales of land, the lower estates had to obtain money through original economic effort. This fostered a new spirit of economic rationalism. Economic households now came to view themselves consciously as 'businesses'. New methods of calculation arose from developments in mathematics in the thirteenth to fifteenth centuries. Leonardo Pisano made available the Indian and Arabic system of numbers, while Luca Paciola created a readily understandable system of double entry bookkeeping. On this basis, Fischer contends that Sombart made clear both the economic origins of the capitalist spirit and the existence of forms of capitalist enterprise long before the period of the Protestant Reformation. A capitalist spirit flourished in medieval Catholic cities such as Genoa, Florence and Venice, as well as in the Papacy's administration of its own assets, and in the lower Rhine area and Catholic Belgium. The Protestant Swiss canton of Bern, on the other hand, developed no capitalist forms. Physical conditions and the 'general state of world trade' may have been more responsible for capitalist development in Holland than Calvinism. Other, non-religious circumstances encouraged a culture of affluence there that had more to do with the fact that few Dutch capitalists cared for the nobility of dormant landed wealth.

Finally, Fischer proposes a more plausible 'psychological' explanation for the rise of capitalist attitudes that makes no appeal to religious consciousness. He argues that Weber's mentality of 'acquiring ever more money as an end in itself' can be seen in terms of 'the pleasure of the individual in active exertion of his powers' (*die Freude des Individuums an seiner kraftvollen Betätigung*). He cites a passage from John Stuart Mill in which Mill describes the origin of the love of money in terms of transference of pleasure in the things money can buy to pleasure in money itself. Money, power and fame gradually cease to be mere means to happiness and instead define our idea of happiness itself. In Fischer's words:

> In our striving for power, fame and money, a transference of feeling-states takes place. The pleasure originally associated with our idea of the *end* (happiness) is transferred to our idea of the *means* (money). Since money is the means of exchange *par excellence*, a transference of this kind will obviously take place in our prizing of money. Religious factors do not affect this process. While the drive to possess money might conceivably rest on religious thought-processes, this way of thinking stems from a reflective psychology [*Reflexionspsychologie*] that makes psychic phenomena appear more complicated than they really are.
>
> (1907:20)

Also citing Herbert Spencer, Fischer proposes that the origin of the capitalist sense of duty in a calling might better be attributed to our association of feelings directed to more distant and generalised goods with a more lasting kind of well-being than feelings requiring immediate satisfaction in the present. Feelings attaching to honesty, charity, thrift and prudence acquire greater authority in our minds than those relating to the lower impulses and desires. Devotion to one's calling ought therefore to be explained less by the negative social sanctions of state and religion than by the positive motive force of pleasure in successful action and lasting self-fulfilment.

CHAPTER 2

Weber's First Reply to Karl Fischer, 1907

From the *Archiv für Sozialwissenschaft und Sozialpolitik*, vol. 25, pp. 243–49

I am grateful to my two co-editors for agreeing to reprint the preceding comments.[i] For however misleading a critical review might be – as I believe the present one is – it always highlights places where misunderstandings are *liable* to arise which the author has not done enough to prevent, whether or not they are actually his fault.

Indeed, with regard to almost all the objections raised by my critic, I must deny any fault on my part, and for some of these I must even reject all possibility of misunderstanding for the attentive reader. Despite my affirming the *contrast* in 'spirit' between the sayings of Jakob Fugger and Benjamin Franklin (XX:15/PE:51), my critic has me finding that spirit equally in *both*.[1][ii] I take Franklin as one of various illustrations for what in an ad hoc way I christened the 'spirit of capitalism' and for this spirit's not being simply linked to *forms of economic enterprise* (XX:26/PE:64f.).[2][iii] Yet my critic thinks I treat Franklin's mental outlook in one place as identical to this capitalist 'spirit' and in another as different from it. I took considerable pains to *demonstrate* that the ethically coloured concept of the 'calling' (and the corresponding verbal meaning), common to *all*

---

[i] Weber's two co-editors were Edgar Jaffé and Werner Sombart. (On the role of Jaffé and Sombart in the *Archiv für Sozialwissenschaft und Sozialpolitik*, see Roth 1992.)

[ii] These sayings are Franklin's 'Remember, that *time* is money' and Fugger's statement that he 'wanted to make money as long as he could' (XX:13, 15/PE:48, 51). At *Archiv* (XX:15/PE:51f.) Weber asserts that 'what in the former case [Fugger] was an expression of commercial daring and a personal inclination morally neutral, in the latter [Franklin] takes on the character of an ethically coloured maxim for the conduct of life. The concept "spirit of capitalism" is here used in this specific sense ...'

[iii] Weber is referring to his distinction between the capitalist 'spirit' or 'ethos' and actual capitalist institutions and structures. Franklin, he notes, 'was filled with the spirit of capitalism at a time when his printing business did not differ in *form* from any handicraft enterprise' (XX:26/PE:64f.).

31

Protestant peoples since the Bible translations but lacking among *all* others, was, in the respect crucial to my investigation, an *invention* of the Reformation (XX:36/PE:79). Yet my critic thinks Luther must have taken up an 'expression familiar to the people' already – though of course he fails to substantiate this 'familiarity' with a single fact. Philological findings may obviously correct my conclusions at any time. However, as the evidence stands, this certainly cannot be done merely by asserting the opposite.

Furthermore, despite my trying to establish at length how and why the idea of the 'calling' in its Lutheran form *differed* in kind from its shape in 'ascetic' Protestantism, where it formed an integral constituent [*integrierender Bestandteil*] of the capitalist 'spirit', my critic presents this difference as an objection to me, when it was my own conclusion and a fundamental argument of my essay. He even accuses me of an 'idealist interpretation of history', deriving capitalism from Luther. I emphatically rejected any such 'foolish' thesis that the Reformation created the capitalist spirit *on its own*, 'or even' the economic *system* of capitalism (XX:54/PE:91).[iv] Important *forms* of capitalist *enterprise* do, of course, considerably pre-date the Reformation. Yet I still do not escape the fate of having this last completely undeniable fact cited *against* me by appeal to my friend Sombart.[v] And whereas I unambiguously protested against using the historical connections I discussed to construct any kind of 'idealist' (in my words 'spiritualist') interpretation of history (XXI:110/PE:183), my critic not only imputes just such an interpretation to me in the above remarks but even considers whether I imagine the transformation of the Baptist ethic as a 'logical process in Hegel's sense.'[3] Once again, he presents to me as his opinion things which I myself said clearly enough for everyone in the relevant place (XXI:69/PE:149).[vi] I do not feel myself to blame if he fails to find plausible the explanation I gave both there and elsewhere for the Baptist atmosphere of life gradually accommodating itself to the 'world' [*für das Einmünden der täuferischen Lebensstimmung in die 'Welt'*].[vii] Such an

---

[iv] The quotation marks in this sentence are for words originally used by Weber, not Fischer. Weber is quoting himself from *Archiv* (XX:54/PE:91).

[v] Sombart 1902.

[vi] At *Archiv* (XXI:69/PE:149) Weber points out that already in the first generation of the Baptist movement 'the strictly apostolic way of life was not maintained as absolutely essential to the proof of rebirth' and that 'well-to-do bourgeois' members numbered among these groups 'even before Menno, who definitely defended the practical worldly virtues and the system of private property.' (Note: Following Parsons, 'Baptist movement' is here used to translate Weber's generic term *Täufertum*. It does not just refer to the post-seventeenth century English and American Baptists.)

[vii] Weber's explanation for the Baptists' return to worldly society was that the belief that 'God speaks only when the flesh is silent' 'meant an incentive to the deliberate weighing-up of courses of action and their careful justification in terms of the individual conscience' (XXI:69/PE:149). 'Hand in hand with this went accommodation to work in a calling' (XXI:69).

explanation is known to hold very well for other sects similar to the Baptists in this respect, for example some Russian sects, which otherwise lived under quite different economic conditions.[4]

Neither do I believe I am responsible if my critic thinks I wrote my essays solely to explain connections still noticeable *today* between confessional allegiances and social–economic stratification. Actually, I stressed very emphatically (XX:23/PE:62, and throughout) that today's mechanically based capitalism that imports Polish workers to Westfalia and coolies to California shows an absolutely different attitude towards that problem from early capitalism.[viii] The fact that differences of economic attitude can nonethelesss still be observed today and are occasionally openly discussed as such merely provided me with a point of departure. It gave me a reason for showing there was at least a legitimate *question* about how religious confession and economic behaviour might have related to each other during capitalism's early period (XX:25/PE:63).

Now it is *a priori* self-evident from the manner in which historically complex occurrences can be causally attributed to each other that, neither today nor in the past, have these two cultural components stood in a relation of 'lawful' interdependence, such that wherever x existed (ascetic Protestantism), there also, without exception, was y (capitalist 'spirit').[5] My critic's remarks about the Dutch capitalists are, in any case, not even factually correct: purchase of manorial lands by certain strata of the urban patriciate was typical there too [not only in England] (XXI:103, n.73/PE:278, n.88).[ix] I briefly discussed the factors determining Holland's development at *Archiv* (XX:26, n.1/PE:200, n.23; XXI:85f/PE:162f.) and intend to return to this issue in more detail later.[x] My comments there were

---

[viii] At *Archiv* (XX:23/PE:61f.) Weber remarks that while capitalism today appears to recruit its labour-force in all industrial regions comparatively easily without the alliance of religion, lasting industrial productivity is unlikely to be secured through either low or high wages but rather through 'a developed feeling of responsibility', the sense of work as 'an absolute end in itself, a calling'.

[ix] Fischer referred to Dutch capitalists having large quantities of capital at their disposal without investing in land as evidence of a general culture of affluence and consumption in Holland that was neither hindered nor encouraged by Calvinism (*Archiv*, XXV:241). At *Archiv* (XX:103, n.73/PE:278, n.88) Weber also notes that 'English Mercantilist writers of the seventeenth century attributed the superiority of Dutch capital to English to the circumstance that newly acquired wealth there did not regularly seek investment in land.' However, he points out that among the bourgeois patricians of the Dutch cities a distinct class of regents emerged who were once merchants but who in the later seventeenth century began to purchase landed estates. 'In this case,' he writes, 'the power of hereditary moneyed property broke through the ascetic spirit'.

[x] At *Archiv* (XX:26, n.1/PE:200, n.23) Weber accepts that the largest moneyed interests in Holland were originally Arminian, not Calvinist. Nonetheless, those who 'were for the most part here and elsewhere typical representatives of capitalist ethics and Calvinist religion' were the smaller traders of the rising bourgeoisie.

highly provisional; yet my critic now likewise uses them in part as an objection to me. The significance of certain religious groups for the development of the Rhine area in the Low Countries during capitalism's early period will probably be discussed in the continuation of my account.[6] It must not be forgotten here, incidentally, that 'Reformed' does not just mean the same as 'Calvinist', and that Calvinism – as I have stressed repeatedly – by no means always reflected the actual teaching of Calvin, and further that even Calvinism did not fully reveal the characteristics I see as relevant to my discussion until it developed into ascetic Protestantism. I refer again emphatically to my comments at *Archiv* (XXI:103f./PE:174f.).[xi] I can scarcely be taken to hold that the mere fact of confessional affiliation will alone conjure up a particular kind of economic development – as if Siberian Baptists were bound to become wholesalers, or Sahara-dwelling Calvinists manufacturers. It would be as absurd to think that Calvinism should have created capitalist forms of enterprise in a country with the geographic and cultural conditions of Hungary during the time of its periodic subjugation by the Turks as that it could have made coal seams form in the soil of Holland. In point of fact, Calvinism did have an effect in Hungary in its own way, although this was in a different field. At *Archiv* (XX:4, n.1&2/PE:188f, n.8&9) I referred to figures showing that the characteristic phenomena I took as my starting-point concerning choice of vocation among Protestants seem to have appeared even in that country.[xii] As for my view of the relations between religious and economic conditions in general, I think I have expressed myself clearly enough on this for the moment, however briefly (XXI:101, n.69/PE:277f., n.84).[xiii] I cannot help it if statements like these, especially my concluding remarks at the end of the entire essay, are simply not heeded.

I do not, therefore, accept responsibility for the misunderstandings I believe underlie the present 'critique.' However, in the separate edition of the essay, which for technical reasons of the publisher's cannot be delayed any longer, I will try once again to remove any phrase which could possibly be understood as

---

[xi] At *Archiv* (XX:103f./PE:174f.) Weber stresses Puritan conduct of life, rather than Calvinist doctrine *per se*. The temptations of wealth that were the unintended consequence of such conduct clearly contradicted Calvinist doctrine.

[xii] This refers to the higher percentage of Protestants compared with Catholics in Hungary attending technical schools oriented to industrial and commercial occupations.

[xiii] At *Archiv* (XXI:101, n.69/PE:277f., n.84) Weber states that while he considers 'the influence of economic development on the fate of religious ideas to be very important', promising in later work 'to show how ... the process of mutual adaptation of the two took place', 'religious ideas ... simply cannot be deduced from economic circumstances. They are in themselves ... the most powerful plastic elements of national character, and contain a law of development and a compelling force entirely their own'.

suggesting a derivation (*Ableitung*) of economic forms from religious motives, which is something I never maintained. Wherever possible, I will try to make even clearer that what I sought to 'derive' from asceticism in its Protestant recasting was the spirit of 'methodical' *conduct of life*, and that this spirit stands only in a relation of 'adequacy' [*Adäquanz*] to economic forms – yet a relation I believe to be of the greatest importance for our cultual history. I am grateful to my critic for prompting me to this. However, when dealing with endlessly entwined causal relationships such as these, substantively fruitful criticism is possible only on the basis of mastery of the source material, which is something he lacks.[7]

Regretfully, I can find no use whatsoever for my critic's more positive, 'psychological' comments. When I argued that the present stock of reliable concepts in psychology was insufficient to be applied safely to a concrete problem in religious history, such as the meaning of certain 'hystericising' processes in early Pietism (XXI:45, n.79a/PE:244, n.114), I was clearly not speaking of the kind of efforts practised by my critic but of the *exact* research on hysteria. If there are any new and valuable insights to be gained in this problem, I shall expect them *only* from research of this nature.[8][xiv] By contrast, what my critic proposes in his review shows me only how useless such 'psychology' remains for historical explanation of the kind of phenomena I was dealing with. 'If', he writes, 'we adopt a psychological account of the acquisition of money ..., viewed purely as an end in itself, we can understand it in terms of the pleasure of the individual in active exertion of his powers.'[9] Viewed historically, this very first step into 'psychology' is already a false one. This 'pleasure in actively exerting oneself' might aptly describe some of the attitudes that accompany the acquisition of money among many modern types of business people, as well as the likes of Jakob Fugger and other similar economic 'supermen' of the past. I have occasionally written about such types myself (XXI:109, n.85a/PE:283, n.115).[10][xv] However, while such types of people have always existed since ancient Babylon wherever it was possible to accumulate money, they emphatically do *not* characterise that spirit of *sober methodical* conduct of life I sought to analyse. One can study the 'active exertion of the individual' and

---

[xiv] At *Archiv* (XXI:45, n.79a/PE:244, n.114) Weber writes: 'The firmly established results of psychology, including psychiatry, do not as present go far enough to make them of use for the purposes of the historical investigation of our problems without prejudicing historical judgements. The use of its terminology would only form a temptation to hide phenomena which were immediately understandable, or even trivial, behind a veil of foreign words, and thus give a false impression of scientific exactitude ...'. Hysteria in Pietism is a special case because it requires both historical understanding of religious concepts and a specific psychological expertise different from the common-sense psychological propositions Fischer has in mind.

[xv] *Archiv* (XXI:109, n.85a/PE:283, n.115) describes a 'leading dry-goods man of an Ohio city' constantly bent on widening his shop frontage.

his 'pleasure' in it in so-called 'Renaissance man'; but if one applies this same expression to the Puritans, who were ascetically reigned-in like monks, one implies two fundamentally different things – hardly surprising given such an imprecise abstraction. My critic's subsequent remarks only show me that generalising doctrines of this kind stand worlds apart from the phenomena of historical reality – whether they concern (i) which scheme of psychological phenomena this 'pleasure' falls under; (ii) whether a certain kind of 'transference of feeling-states' takes place as a 'general psychical occurrence', and what the theoretical import of this is; (iii) which historical processes are in consequence 'conceivable'; (iv) when the attitude of 'prizing money' could have arisen and when not (noting, as I stress again, that this notion obviously covers a quite heterogeneous range of mentalities, from Molière's 'miser'[xvi] to Carnegie and the Indian Rajah, and has nothing in itself to do with Puritan methodical conduct of life);[11] or finally (v) how one might try to explain the abstractness and origin of the concept of 'sense of duty' and account in particular for the origin of 'duty in a calling' in a more 'natural' way than myself. I have explained the fundamental methodological errors of these doctrines so many times already, I can spare myself the repetition here.[xvii]

Certainly, it would be considerably easier for our discovery of the historical causal chain if we could simply deduce the emergence of certain unique stylisations of life from the abstractions of a 'psychology.' However, historical reality does not allow itself to be dictated to. History does not care that it may be tiresome for the psychological schemas of a John Stuart Mill, a Herbert Spencer[12] or even my critic that past peoples entertained very concrete ideas about what awaited them after their death and the means of improving their prospects therein, and that they determined their behaviour accordingly. For it cannot be gainsaid that the way our forebears' different views about the requirements of salvation influenced their different behaviours was of the utmost importance for cultural development – however difficult it may be for us modern people to imagine ourselves in the harrowing power of those metaphysical ideas.

Still, after all his various 'psychological' reflections, my critic does finally acknowledge a clear connection between the development of the capitalist 'spirit' in France and the Huguenot movement. Although he thinks this 'parallel' remains quite inexplicable, I flatter myself that I have (i) made its existence probable for a number of other regions as well, and (ii) made a reasonably plausible attempt at explaining it through a series of at least noteworthy facts. Whether the abstractions of a 'psychology' fit the facts I have presented or not, I frankly do not care:

[xvi] From Molière's play of 1668, *L'Avare*.
[xvii] See Weber 1904; 1905a.

theory must follow the facts, not vice versa. I welcome the assistance of psychology wherever its concepts help me to attribute concrete historical occurrences to their concrete causes. But for my *particular* problem, I see nothing of consequence in what I know of the 'psychological' literature, including the works cited by my critic. And so far as the questions that interest me are concerned, precise scientific research on religious pathology still remains unfortunately in its infancy.

Weber's Notes

1   And moreover, he cites *only* these two sayings. One will surely have to grant me that at *Archiv* (XX:18–35/PE:55–78) I have provided a little more clarification of this concept [of the 'spirit of capitalism'], however provisional.

2   For the reverse case of this, see my remarks at *Archiv* (XX:28/PE:66f).[xviii]

3   Of course, just like early Christianity, the original partly eschatological, partly 'enthusiastic' and partly anti-political ethic of the Baptist movement developed along a course of 'adaptation to the world' (*Anpassung an die Welt*), as I myself expressed it. This has long been known, and I myself have spoken clearly enough about it. But this was not: adaptation to *capitalism*. The Baptist movement's first decisive 'adaptation to the world' took place predominantly in regions like Friesland which lagged way behind other areas in capitalist development.

4   On just one point, a printing error may have been at fault, though it should have been very easily recognisable as such. Concerning the Anabaptists, the text at *Archiv* (XXI:69/PE:149) runs: 'Of course, this waiting might result in hysterical conditions, prophecy and ... under certain circumstances even in an outbreak of chiliastic enthusiasm, as was the case with the movement destroyed in Münster'. A printing error made 'result in hysterical conditions' [*in hysterische Zustände ... ausmünden*] into 'waiting in hysterical conditions' [*dieses Harrens in hysterischen Zuständen*]. To my mind, the sense of the sentence itself, and definitely the subsequent remarks, reveal at first glance that it is a printing error. What could one possibly understand by '*waiting* in hysterical conditions' – something that obviously contradicts the idea of sober work in a calling, as my critic points out?[xix]

5   The *only* imprudent formulation one might censure was my remark at *Archiv* (XX:8/PE:43) that Calvinism showed the conjunction of intense piety with capitalist business acumen 'wherever it appeared'. I was thinking there of the Calvinist diaspora, which Gothein also discusses at the place I then cited.[xx]

[xviii]   Weber means enterprise in which use of capital and rational bookkeeping was indispensable but whose spirit remained 'traditionalistic', for example the putting-out system in mid-nineteenth-century textile industries on the European continent.

[xix]   Weber's complaint in this note is that by not recognising the anomalous switch from accusative to dative case in the 'n' at the end of *Zuständen*, Fischer appears to have missed both the concessive force of Weber's reference to hysteria-outbursts, as a qualifying rather than directly supporting part of his argument, and also, more importantly, his point that what was important was less Baptist theology than the 'specifically methodical character of Baptist morality', the ethos of waiting for the descent of the Holy Spirit in order 'to overcome everything impulsive and irrational, the passions and subjective interests of the natural man' (XXI:68f./PE:148 [trans. modified]) and the Baptists' gradual reincorporation of this ethos into worldly society.

[xx]   At *Archiv* (XX:8/PE:43), Weber quotes Gothein's description of the Calvinist diaspora as the 'seed-bed of capitalist economy' in Gothein (1892, vol. I:67). Eberhard Gothein (1853–1923): historian, economist and political scientist, professor at Karlsruhe, Bonn and Heidelberg.

6   Of course, for the *present* development of this region, only what I said about *contemporary* capitalism applies. This is so especially for Belgium *today*. By contrast, in the sixteenth century, those Calvinists who initially moved into the southern Belgian area, where they were a minority, but then gradually migrated northwards into Holland, were of the greatest importance, both political and economic, as any history of the Thirty Years War demonstrates.

7   I would expect the most competent criticism to come from a *theological direction* – however 'backward' some may regard this.

8   Such research *may* also shed light on the influence of religious institutions and ideas on all that we lump together today under the empty concept of 'national character'. More on this too when the separate edition brings the opportunity.

9   Here he again quotes that saying of Fugger's that I had *contrasted* with what I called 'capitalist spirit'. As far as *terminology* is concerned, I would always be prepared to exchange this term for a more suitable one. However, he then also refers to the 'capitalist spirit' in Florence, despite my plainly setting out the *differences* of the medieval attitude from what *I* mean by 'capitalist spirit' (XX:32/PE:73). If one *ignores* these specific differences, the meaning of the concept will indeed be lost.

10   One hardly need mention that this type exists not only in its pure American form but that there is also something of it among wide strata of the entrepreneurial classes today.

11   See *Archiv* (XX:19/PE:56) and the whole second half of Part II (PE:155f.).

12   The 'explanatory theories' my critic invokes in these two distinguished scholars are specifically English in character, and in part themselves late expressions of that 'natural' outlook on life that we also find in Franklin. Yet they represent the very reverse of empirical historical inquiry. The only shreds of validity in such constructs are a few commonplaces of everyday experience, with which all economic historians constantly operate without needing to read Mill or Spencer.

Part II

CHAPTER 3

Karl Fischer's Reply to Weber, 1908

From the *Archiv für Sozialwissenschaft und Sozialpolitik*, vol. 26, pp. 270–74

Summary

Fischer maintains that Weber's 'temperamental' response has missed the crux of the issue. He denies assuming either that Weber sought to explain presently existing connections between religious confession and socio-economic position or that what Weber sought to 'derive' from religious motives were the material–economic forms and structures of capitalist enterprise. Weber, he complains, has ascribed to him the most unfavourable position: he fully understood that what Weber sought to 'derive' from Protestant asceticism was the 'spirit of methodical conduct of life' and that Weber only wished to consider those cases where religious influences on material culture were truly indisputable.

However, Fischer still declares himself unhappy with Weber's method, insisting that however much Weber may deny substituting a 'one-sidedly intellectualist' interpretation of historical causation for a 'one-sidedly materialist' one, he does not actually live up to this claim. Fischer's central contention is that we can speak of 'the', or at least 'a', spirit of methodical conduct of life long before the rise of Puritanism. The question at issue for him is not whether Puritan attitudes influenced and reinforced the spirit of methodical conduct of life *once it had arisen*, but what caused it to arise in the first place:

> There is no doubt that once the religious–economic outlook of Puritanism had emerged, it strengthened the spirit of methodical conduct of life wherever this spirit was not yet greatly developed. However, the issue lies not with the interaction of these two elements, which no one denies, but the with the *genesis* of the spirit of methodical conduct of life in this period.

> (1908:40)

He then reiterates that Lutheranism's emphasis on duty in a calling as the highest moral activity and Calvinism's perception of successful labour as a sign of election can only have resulted from adaptation to prevalent economic circumstances. Weber's discussion of theological devotional literature, on the other hand, shows at most that the authors of these texts allowed economic beliefs to become woven into their dogmatic systems. In Fischer's view, Weber shows that both factors, the religious and economic, were present simultaneously and closely bound up with each other, but nothing more than this. He has not proved decisively that the spirit of methodical conduct of life arose exclusively from religious motives because he has not refuted alternative explanations:

> To make this conclusion compelling, one would have to demonstrate that in every single case other interpretations are excluded. One would have to show that no spirit of methodical conduct of life appeared before the emergence of Puritan religious literature, whether in earlier religious literature or secular thought.

> (1908:41)

Finally, returning to methodology, Fischer argues that since we cannot perform experiments on history whenever we try to reach judgement on the motives of past actors, we must fall back on psychological interpretations. Consciously or not, we always possess an 'epistemological standpoint' of some kind on what happens in our surrounding world. Therefore, in historical research, we must make ourselves aware of what implicit psychological presuppositions we hold. He queries why Weber countenances psychological research on hysteria in history but not psychological thought in general, least of all when this concerns his central theme of methodical conduct of life. Parrying Weber's complaint that 'theory must follow the facts, not vice versa' and that Fischer lacks adequate knowledge of the period and its sources, Fischer retorts:

> [A] substantively fruitful critique ... should be especially concerned to evaluate its source material in a way that is not methodologically objectionable. In particular, it should be aware that our very knowledge and assessment of historical objects is not possible without certain – I am sorry to say – *psychological* presuppositions.

> (1908:43).

CHAPTER 4

Weber's Second Reply to Karl Fischer, 1908

From the *Archiv für Sozialwissenschaft und Sozialpolitik*, vol. 26, pp. 275–83

A reader who wanted to get to grips with this (not very fruitful) reply would have to be not only 'thoughtful', but above all *patient* enough to refer to *my* essay on every point to find out what I said and what I omitted to say. He would surely then be astonished at the claim that I had not 'seen' the elementary 'methodological' principles and problems of historical causation that my critic presents to me above in this patronising way. And he would be astonished that I had *therefore* 'offered nothing' by way of reflection on the decisive causal questions of my study. This claim is all the more astonishing in view of the purely aprioristic way my critic believes he can treat these problems himself, knowing as he does absolutely *nothing* about the matter in question – not even the most general literary characteristics of the sources. In his supposedly 'methodological' remarks, he calls them 'books of religious devotion' and then confuses these with 'dogmatic systems'. Here he lacks knowledge of the *subject-matter*. He simply does not know that the decisive sources for my account of the influences on conduct of life (alongside other sources which I used only where a concrete question demanded them) arose from collections of responses relating directly to quite concrete practical questions posed to the clergy (at that time the most universal counsellors any epoch has known). These sources had nothing whatever to do with 'devotional or 'dogmatic' purposes but much more with problems of how to organise one's daily life [*Problemen der alltäglichen Lebensgestaltung*], which they illustrate like few other sources. His 'methodological' views on what a literature completely unfamiliar to him can at 'at most' prove, and what not, must therefore be of little significance. And if he pronounces as inconsequential on grounds of 'generality' my remark about modern people's difficulty imagining themselves dealing with practical questions of life of that time and the way these were influenced by religious motives, I will gladly rephrase my remark: I will state more precisely that *he* undoubtedly lacks this ability. However, I scarcely still dare hope to win him over to my views. For his question of *why*, despite plausible reasons, one ought to resist recognising such an influence (in the way I have portrayed it), is, for him personally, very easy to answer. Clearly, his firm conviction of *himself* possessing an infinitely simple means of determining historical 'psychogeneses' – in the form of what he calls 'psychology' – cannot have aided the impartiality of his judgement on what he contends are the all too complicated labours of others. One does not need the help of 'psychology' to see this.[i]

A discussion that is not based on *some* knowledge of the subject cannot by any means pretend to represent a 're-examination' of historical investigations, even with the best of 'methodological' intentions. For, instead of the allegedly 'methodological' claims, we are here presented constantly with *factual* ones, claims moreover that are tossed out at random and based on ignorance. Assertions such as that an 'adaptation' of the religious imagination to given existing economic circumstances must be 'supposed', as well as all similar phrases, are clearly *substantive* in nature. Given that such questions have already been addressed under precisely this aspect in a not inconsiderable body of literature (which includes such diverse writers as Kautsky and Dilthey),[ii] my critic's assertions clearly fall far short of the current historical debate from which I set out, and are in any case quite devoid of content.[1] And, above all, they simply ignore the fact that I do not *at all* consider settled the question of the influence of economic processes on religious movements by my conclusions to date on the direction taken by the *reverse* influence. I made this clear both in explicit statements and in the whole structure of my investigation. My critic seems to think he can simply ignore my statements as irrelevant, on the grounds that I have not (indeed, have nowhere) acted in accordance with them. *This* allegation, however, he has never attempted to substantiate through analysis of my argument. Instead, he just 'insists' on certain *'words'* – or more accurately 'fixates' ['*klammert*'] on them. In particular, he fixes on the expression 'derive' [*ableiten*] (which I not unintentionally put in inverted commas). This refers to my derivation of the vocational ethic from Protestant asceticism, and certain economically relevant components of the modern lifestyle from this 'vocational ethic'. What I mean by this term 'derive' should be clear to any *reader* of my essay. But even to a non-reader, it really is apparent enough from the *words* quoted by my critic three lines

---

[i]   Weber means: one does not need to use psychology on Fischer himself to see how tendentious he has been.

[ii] For Weber's relation to Dilthey, see Rossi 1994; Harrington 2000, 2001; for Kautsky, see *Archiv* XX: /PE:258, n.188.

later (concerning the *'influence'* of religious consciousness on cultural life) that it was not my concern to discover 'the motive factor of historical change' in any epoch or some *'truly* driving forces' – because for me phantoms like these do not exist in history. Rather, my stated intention was to investigate in what direction the religious peculiarities of the various ascetic Protestant movements and the fundamental metaphysical beliefs underpinning them influenced conduct of life – wherever such an influence occurred *at all*. Yet my critic offers not the slightest evidence for his audacious assumption that I was nonetheless undertaking an idealist interpretation of history. It was precisely against this unsubstantiated charge of acting contrary to my intentions that I lodged what he calls my 'temperamental' riposte.

As for the claim that I failed in any way to consider *other*, especially economic, kinds of motive, need I make it still clearer for *readers* of my essay how still more audacious this claim is? I would simply remind them of the following. For reasons given earlier, my view is that the *degree* of religious influence was often *very* great. I did not prove that it was everywhere *equally* great, nor that it could not have been weakened or completely outweighed by other circumstances – but neither did I ever claim this. What I did provide evidence for – and this was my sole concern – was that the *direction* taken by the religious influence in Protestant countries of the most varied political, economic, geographical and ethnic conditions imaginable was, in all crucial respects, the *same* – whether in New England, the German diaspora, southern France, Holland or England. (And the Irish 'Scotch-Irish', Friesland and numerous other German regions could have been added here.) In particular, I justified my contention that this direction remained *independent* of the degree of capitalist development as an *economic system*. I also pointed out that even in the region of highest capitalist development *before* the Reformation, namely Italy (and Flanders also), there was no 'capitalist *spirit*' in *my* sense of this word. This, as I merely indicate here, had the most far-reaching consequences for 'style of life'.[2] Some may attack my evidence for the religious character of ascetic Protestantism having a *uniform* tendency to influence behaviour as incomplete or as demonstrated only to a certain degree of probability, or they may attack it on *substantive* grounds (in particular, theological grounds). But at all events, considering (1) my line of reasoning, (2) my related repeated remarks about the *meaning* of my thesis and (3) my statements about future investigations for completing, interpreting and testing it further,[3] one will understand why I had to answer my critic 'temperamentally' and uncompromisingly, and why I found, and still find, rather thoughtless the opinion he now expressly voices that I had not 'seen' those actually quite simplistic 'methodological' principles of which he speaks and that I offer no methodological *'considerations'* whatever of this nature in my work.[4] What I find absent, both in his original review and here, is not only any knowledge of the subject but also the 'goodwill' to look clearly at something before dismissing it. If the holy and so 'proper'[iii] 'methodological' zeal of my critic now says I should have been expected to exclude *'every possibility'* of a different causal linkage, so that no interpretation would have been left permissible and 'conceivable' other than my own, the historian, for well-known reasons, will unfortunately scarcely be able to recognise such a negative burden of proof as a *general* 'norm' of his conduct. Normally he will work the other way round, investigating the effects of the *other* causal components positively [the economic, political components etc.]. In this way, he will arrive at an ever more comprehensive (but never entirely self-sufficient) attribution of causes – just as (I repeat again) I said *expressly* it was my intention and had begun to carry out anyway in my articles so far.

Above all, however, that ideal yardstick my critic uses to measure the force of *others'* explanations contrasts all too strongly with the modesty of the demands he places on his *own* arguments. Consider his desire to 'demonstrate'(!) the respective 'psychogeneses' of 'duty in a calling', the 'capitalist spirit' and the 'spirit of methodical conduct of life'. How (in 10 pages) has he managed to achieve this task when he assures us both that it is extremely difficult and that I myself completely failed in it? In his review, he spoke of 'advancing' 'beyond' Sombart and myself to a higher synthesis, i.e. 'to the psychological explanation' of these developments (*Archiv*, XXV:238).[5] Let us recall his words: 'If we adopt a *psychological account* of the acquisition of money ... viewed purely as an end in itself, we can understand it in terms of the pleasure of the individual in active exertion of his powers ... This pleasure in active exertion is in no way religiously conditioned; it is linked directly to the activity' (*Archiv*, XXV:239). (Readers are welcome to consult his discoveries of a similar quality regarding the 'psychogenesis' of the sense of duty and, in particular, of duty in a calling, which he thinks arose because 'the idea of fulfilling one's vocation possessed greater validity than that of not pursuing a vocation', rather like poverty arising from 'destitution'.)[iv] My critic is right: these dicta do not deserve the names I gave them of 'abstractions' and 'psychological schemata'; they are a harmless playing around with definitions, from which things are then deduced, no matter whether the point of the phenomenon so 'defined' is thereby obscured – I showed this in my First Reply, as far as seemed necessary. But if he now takes these generalisations from imprecisely described everyday truisms and sets them up in all seriousness as 'historical *psychology*', all serious psychologists will surely smile at these generalisations today – just as do

---

[iii] An ironic play on the two meanings of *billig*: the older meaning of 'proper' and the more recent, familiar meaning of 'cheap'.
[iv] Weber is ridiculing the tautology in Fischer's assertion.

we present-day economists at his quotation from J.S. Mill.[v] Mill's remarks about the historical emergence of the mentality of prizing money from its putatively original form in the concept of a mere 'means to happiness' may certainly have been 'excellent' in their day, but they are really rather outdated today – though admittedly I have neither sought to disprove them, nor feel tempted to do so here. In the closing sentence of my reply, I speculated that exact research on the *pathology of religion* in particular might one day throw light on certain problems (and not simply research on hysteria *tout court*, as my critic reports it).[6] There I hinted at something which every informed person knows: that despite all its rashness and imperfections, the kind of 'psychology of religion' that treats the 'experiential' and irrational element in religious life as a 'pathological process' promises to deliver more in future (and in some cases already has) to illuminate the relevant '*characterological*' effects of certain kinds of piety than 'quite ordinary' theologians are capable of. For *my* problems it is of course *these* questions that matter. Naturally, I will certainly not stray too close to real '*exact* normal psychology'. However, I think the most a psychology of the type my critic's remarks portray can achieve in this field is – to expose itself as it deserves.

I would scarcely have dwelt so long on all these things if it had not again become clear how the superstitious belief in a quite specific importance of psychology for history (which fortunately some of precisely the most eminent psychologists *no longer* share) serves both to compromise the impartiality of historical research and, frankly, to discredit scientific psychology (for whose achievements in the field of its *own* problems I have the greatest respect), making the historian mistrustful of its assistance even where he has every reason to seek its advice – which doubtless happens not infrequently. I too have been obliged simply to ridicule the supposedly 'psychologically' founded 'historical laws' of a man of such merit in his own field as Wundt[vi] – and I believe with reason and results. Unfortunately, we know what happened when a writer who once bequeathed us *Deutsches Wirtschaftsleben im Mittelalter* attempted to make this so-called 'psychology' usable for history (and after it several other psychologies of the most varying provenance).[vii] I will return to this elsewhere. The findings of professional psychology are occasionally relevant to history in *exactly* the same way as those of astronomy, sociology, chemistry, legal dogmatics, theology, mechanical engineering, anthropology, and so on. The lay belief that because

---

[v]   See Part I, summary of Fischer, in this volume, pp.28–29.

[vi] Weber 1905a.

[vii] Karl Lamprecht (1856–1915), author of *Das Deutsche Wirtschaftsleben im Mittelalter* [*German Economic Life in the Middle Ages*], 1886, 3 vols, was a historian and philosopher of history, notably influenced by Wundt's *Völkerpsychologie*. He argued for a theory of history oriented to discerning the 'spirit of the age' of successive epochs in terms of law-like developments in social–psychic forces.

history is concerned with 'mental events' and *so* (as people believe, and as they say in today's popular idiom) 'starts from psychological presuppositions', it must therefore be based to a unique degree on 'psychology', in the sense of a specialist discipline – this belief is about as poorly founded as the assumption that because the great deeds of 'historical personalities' are always bound up with the 'medium' of sound waves or ink, the foundational disciplines for history are acoustics and the physics of fluid dynamics, or that because history is played out on planet earth its foundation must be astronomy, or because it deals with people, anthropology. History – 'I am sorry to say' – makes 'general psychological assumptions' *only* in the sense that it makes general 'astronomical assumptions'. No one who has not thought through this series of apparent 'paradoxes' at least once has the right to pontificate from the high horse of 'epistemological' or 'methodological' pedantry. And when, from a similarly lordly height, my critic thinks he can stress the 'higher standards' he demanded of his 'critique' (as against the lower ones I demanded in the methodology of my own works), I regret to have to reply that even in methodological respects his 'standards' fall short of what *every* writer criticised in a review must expect of a *'critique'*. If, in his forthcoming book, he will furnish us with some arguments that really keep to a field he has command over, instead of rapping the knuckles of others in fields where he lacks sufficient knowledge, he can be sure of the most impartial reception and a more respectful one than I was able to give him here due to the manner of his reasoning – whatever great differences of opinion might still remain between us. Formal 'politeness' will not necessarily exclude presumptuousness in knowledge of the matter at hand. It was just such presumptuousness that underlay *even* the *positive* comments my critic saw fit to include in his 'critique'.[7] These too I cannot accept when they come from an incompetent. (Indeed, here I concur with a remark of the masterly G.F. Knapp, when, after a similar experience, he once said to me: 'Certainly I do not like to read in print that I am an ass. But I am not pleased either if someone feels he has to commit to print that I am *not* an ass'.)[viii]

Weber's Notes

1   Unless we clarify this concept of 'adaptation' precisely, everything is 'adapted' to everything in historical life – or nothing is. Mormonism is 'adapted' to the economic 'conditions' of Utah just as the ways of life of the other Rocky Mountain states were 'adapted'. The Jesuit state in Paraguay was 'adapted' to the rainforest there just as the life of the Indians was before and after it. The economic conduct of life of the Skoptsy,[ix] the Stundists[x] and

---

[viii]   Georg Friedrich Knapp (1842–1926): professor of economics at Strasbourg and Leipzig.

[ix]   The Skoptsy: Russian castration sect, dating from the 1770s.

[x]   The Stundists: Pietist movement among peasants in the Ukraine and southern Russia, influenced by Protestant German settlers there after 1824 and named after the holy 'hours' (*Stunden*) of the Pastor J. Bonekämper.

other sectarians in Russia is 'adapted' to living conditions there just as is the way of life of neighbouring Orthodox peasants. All these three cases are 'adapted', despite marked differences between them. What was *not* adapted to economic conditions when it was first created was Calvin's theocracy in Geneva, if one considers the economic decline (or the noticeable but easily explicable stagnation) that followed in its wake. I could even formulate the theme of my study thus: in *what sense* can we speak of 'adaptation' (of different cultural elements to each other) in these contexts?

2 For example, one perceptive art historian has traced right down to characteristic artistic motifs the significance of precisely that tension between economic *forms* and ethical lifestyle that resulted from the absence of any 'vocational ethic' in my sense of this word among the immortally unique Florentine bourgeoisie.[xi] One has to *know* these (and many other) historical problems and facts before nonchalantly rustling up phrases (again concerning *facts*), such as that methodical conduct of life also 'appeared in the human race' before Puritanism 'of course'(!). Where, please? And what kind of methodical conduct of life? Let me reiterate once and for all that *I* speak of methodical conduct of life *only* in the sense I analysed over several dozen pages of my essay: the sense in which it influenced life as an element of the modern 'vocational ethic'. I do not include the 'methodical' attitude of, say, the Japanese samurai, or the *Cortegiano*,[xii] or chivalric honour in the Middle Ages, or Stoicism, or 'objective treatment' of life in the Renaissance in the sense coined by Jakob Burckhardt, and not even certain ideas of Francis Bacon, who stands halfway between the Renaissance and the Reformation and is in this respect closer to Puritanism, or finally the Counter-Reformation. All these cases certainly had their own specific element of 'method', and for just that reason components of *all* of them have entered the lifestyle of leading modern nations (some of which I shall discuss in due course). However, these are rationalisations of life in quite *different* directions and senses from those with which *I* was concerned. I *expressly* underlined this in my essay for one case relevant to my theme.

3 The reason why I cannot yet embark on these investigations has nothing to do with any difficulties over facts. It is partly due to personal circumstances of no interest here, partly because my other present work concerns matters far removed from the topic (as anyone who has glanced at the *Archiv für Sozialwissenschaft* knows), and finally partly because in the meantime my colleague and friend Ernst Troeltsch has addressed a whole series of problems that lay along my route in a most felicitous way from his own stock of ideas, and so I wished to avoid unnecessary duplication of work (in which he commands far greater specialist knowledge).[xiii] But I hope to come back to this again in the course of the year, and in the meantime check through the essay at least by the spring for a separate edition. This delay admittedly has the disadvantage that hasty readers will easily see the essay as something self-contained. However, this is *no* excuse for the kind of 'critique' I have been confronted with here. My critic had every right to say that the test for a converse causal relationship and more detailed interpretation I *promised* have so far been *lacking*. But it is more than I will stand for to have someone factually quite incompetent impute to me an 'idealist' interpretation of history when I have always protested against this with good reason, and now even to claim outright that I did not even *see* these problems.

[xi]   Weber does not tell us which art historian he means but he is quite probably referring to Karl Neumann (1860–1934), professor of art history at Heidelberg, Göttingen and Kiel. Neumann's book on Rembrandt is cited in a footnote to the second edition of *The Protestant Ethic* (PE:273, n.66).

[xii] Baldassare Castiglione's *Il libro del cortegiano* (*The Book of the Courtier*), 1528, a code of the social skills required by courtiers.

[xiii] Weber is refering to Troeltsch (1906a) and Troeltsch (1906b).

4   Even though I immediately recognised my critic's ignorance of the sources, I recommended acceptance of his review to my co-editors because it raised a number of points and apparent difficulties that I well remembered having *inwardly* debated myself at the time. I wanted to use the opportunity to discuss these points in a way I believed I had not done in the essay itself. But on rereading my essay, I was not a little surprised, and certainly very little pleased, to find that I had already clearly set out *all* these issues and put them in context, from which my 'critic' had then uncritically wrenched them and misunderstood them, due to ignorance of the subject, only to quote them back at me as 'objections'. I regret not having spared the *Archiv* and its readers this worthless discussion. Having once accepted the review, I was forced into a lengthy clarification of the confusion caused by it. If it had appeared elsewhere, I would not have considered it worth an answer.

5   For he maintains that Sombart's account has been 'challenged' – the proof being one of those reviews, equally questionable in form and content, in which Sombart is regularly discussed by Hans Delbrück in the *Preußische Jahrbücher*.[xiv] However, it is precisely this part of Sombart's account – his discourse on the significance of 'calculativeness' (*Rechenhaftigkeit*) and the techniques it involves – that is relatively the least disputed. And as for Sombart's central question of whence arose the modern economic importance of capitalist *industrial* and *commercial* forms, I consider his account completely correct in all crucial respects. To be sure, fully developed manual work brings with it a certain degree of 'rationalisation' of economic activity, and *ancient* forms of capitalist enterprise dating back to the most distant millennia known to us likewise produced 'calculativeness' to a certain degree. But we can leave for discussion elsewhere the question of *why* 'calculativeness' in the capitalist economic forms of antiquity remained so far *below* the level of development reached by early modern forms, despite being at times quite colossal in quantitative terms. This was so much so that Sombart is right to speak of 'capitalism' as an economic stage only in *modern* times, and to distinguish this from individual capitalist *enterprises* – which have been known to exist for 4000 years. It goes without saying that for his *own* central question Sombart considers *technical* 'calculativeness' the decisive characteristic of the 'spirit of capitalism'. For *my* question, to do with the rise of that *ethical* 'lifestyle' that was mentally 'adequate' to the economic stage of 'capitalism' and thereby victorious over the human 'soul', I believe my terminology is justified. We have both been concerned with the same phenomena, but from different angles and with myself necessarily focusing on different features. So it is a matter of terminological differences, not substantive disagreements, at least not on my side. Indeed, as far as I can see, we are entirely at one in our attitude to historical materialism. It is not *my* fault if others have exaggerated the scope of my acknowledgement of 'ideological' causal elements. It is quite possible that once my investigations have come to an end, I shall be accused with just as much indignation of capitulating to historical materialism as I am now to ideology.[xv]

6   I mentioned this in a quite *different* context, to do with certain aspects of Pietism. I find my critic's polemic against me here really quite rich. Even though I pointed out that his comments about 'hysterical states' among the Baptists arose from an obvious misunderstanding, he still repeats his assertion that I 'conceded' I was expecting elucidation of the Baptist movement from research into *hysteria*, and 'wittily' asks whether such research might help to explain the emergence of 'methodical conduct of life'. First, I 'conceded' absolutely *nothing* that was not clearly to be read in my essay; and, second, my critic has not even taken the trouble to look and see what precisely I said could be expected from

---

[xiv]   This refers to Sombart (1902), reviewed by Hans Delbrück in *Preußische Jahrbücher*, vol. 113, 1903, pp.333–50. Hans Delbrück (1848–1929): professor of history at Berlin and editor of the *Preußische Jahrbücher*.
[xv]   'Ideology' here not in the Marxian sense.

research into hysteria, and what not. Clearly, his 'chain of unhappy misunderstandings' remains unbroken – and still for the same reasons as before.

7   Incidentally, that he first awarded my essay epithets such as 'thorough', and similar. when he now thinks it has not 'seen' the simplest causal problems speaks neither for his knowledge of the subject nor, unfortunately, his objectivity.

Part III

CHAPTER 5

Felix Rachfahl's Review of *The Protestant Ethic*, 1909

From the *Internationale Wochenschrift für Wissenschaft, Kunst und Technik*, 1909, 3rd quarter, pp. 1217–1366

Summary

Felix Rachfahl's review is considerably longer than Karl Fischer's, containing some 90 pages, serialised in five parts in the *Internationale Wochenschrift*, 1909, nos. 39–43. It also includes frequent references to Troeltsch's essay on 'Protestant Christianity and the Modern Church' (Troeltsch 1906a) and 'Protestantism and Progress' (Troeltsch 1906b), which Rachfahl sees as broadly co-extensive with Weber's thesis.

Rachfahl sees three areas of difficulty in Weber: (1) problems with the concept of 'capitalist spirit'; (2) Calvinism and the vocational ethic; and (3) the economic influence of Calvinism.

Rachfahl sees Weber's concept of the capitalist spirit as both too wide and too narrow: too wide because it includes all people who break with what Sombart called traditionalistic attitudes and seek more than their immediate needs but who do not actually accumulate capital, typically people of the lower middling strata whose only concern is to improve their social–economic standing; and too narrow because it excludes motives that go beyond acquisition of wealth for its own sake such as honour and respect, well-being for one's family and kin, and power and service to the nation. Rachfahl sees Weber's notion of acquisitiveness underpinned by frugality and abstinence as in practice hard to distinguish from miserliness. Any concept of the capitalist spirit ought also to include an element of calculative expenditure and speculation. Rachfahl contends that Weber's unnecessary restrictions stem from his use of ideal-types which invidiously rule out alternative causal scenarios and from his abstract opposition of the capitalist spirit to traditionalist need-based economies. This opposition wrongly includes actors who demonstrate no major break with traditionalism in terms of income and wrongly excludes actors who, while no Puritans, accumulate large amounts of capital.

With regard to Calvinism, Rachfahl stresses that while Calvin's attitudes to economic life and usury in particular were more liberal than Luther's, Calvin emphatically placed charity above private gain. Although usury was not wrong in itself for Calvin, no business was to be made of it. Interest had to be accompanied by restrictions wherever the welfare of the community was at stake. And whatever relaxation of the ban on interest occurred in this period was not due to Calvin's teaching but had begun already. Calvin condemned the amassing of riches for its own sake and would have preferred that people remain in poverty, obedient and aware of their duties to God, than profit from their labour. Thus this Calvinist 'infusion of work with the spirit of Christian morality' could have only hindered capitalist development. It certainly cannot explain the subsequent growth of banks and companies.

Rachfahl finds particular trouble with Weber's concept of 'inner-worldly asceticism'. Essentially, he questions whether rationalised conduct of life and self-discipline should properly be called asceticism. For if, he argues, asceticism is not to be defined too broadly in a way that makes it no different from general piety, it must involve renunciation of material life through flight from the world; but this was only properly achieved in the monastic orders of the Middle Ages:

> Certainly Calvinist ethics in its teaching and practice shows various elements of a turning away from the world and hostility to some material goods. We can call these features 'ascetic' insofar as they are already inherent elements of medieval Catholic asceticism; but they justify no talk of asceticism in the sense of a fully developed style of conduct of life unless bound up with principled flight from the world and a particular kind of deliberate action ... If we are to call the Calvinist vocational ethic 'asceticism', we must never forget that it is quite incommensurable with Catholic asceticism, whose most consistent expression is monasticism, and is unconnected to it other than by name – a name it would consequently be best to discard.

(1909:92–93)

Rachfahl maintains that Weber's and Troeltsch's account of the economic consequences of Calvinism is 'often ambivalent, vague and contradictory' and in need of more exact corroboration. He notes that commercial and industrial life took off in France between 1450 and 1550, before the emergence of the Huguenots, especially under Louis XI, in the silk and metal industries and at the Lyon stock exchange, and resolutely continued during the persecution of the Huguenots under Louis XIV. Much of the Low Countries' wealth was established before the arrival of Calvinism, and much of Dutch wealth came originally from

Flemish immigrants. Competition caused by this immigration fed Amsterdam's commercial vitality and led to the breaking away of a native capitalist clique from Arminianism to Calvinism. Until then, Amsterdam remained faithful to the Spanish empire because the leading aristocracy of the city were Catholic, while all Antwerp bankers were mild Catholics. Orthodox Calvinism's victory in Amsterdam was short-lived, closely bound up with political factionalism, and generally outweighed by confessional indifference among the majority of the population, while trade with Catholic Spain continued unabated.

English Protestantism may have more likely acted as a useful pharisaical prick of conscience for already established capitalists than a positive driving force. Most English economic expansion took place under colonisation and industrialisation in a later era of religious liberalism and rationalism exemplified by latitudinarianism, deism and scepticism. Therefore, to ascribe all these movements to secularisation of the vocational ethic would be an 'exaggeration'. American capitalism did not take off until the late eighteenth century, and did so mainly thanks to a secular rationalist spirit, not Puritanism; while in many parts of North America until then, transactions were more or less in barter form. Conversely, the episcopal southern States were renowned for grand business projects and plantations but were few in Protestants.

Essentially, Rachfahl argues that Weber is wrong to exclude Renaissance and late-medieval developments from the 'capitalist spirit'. Renaissance capitalists such as Fugger fundamentally broke with economic traditionalism, and in doing so they possessed a definite ethics of economic life:

> Fugger's pronouncements show that he was not 'traditionalist' in outlook: he wanted to earn more than he needed; he sought profit for profit's sake; and he spurned all enjoyment without the labour of business. How can this not constitute an ethical maxim for the conduct of life? How can Weber know that Fugger did not feel himself inwardly beholden to his vocation, that he too might have felt himself placed before a duty of life to fulfill his mission faithfully and conscientiously?

> (1909:108)

Rachfahl maintains that 'vocation' and 'vocational ethics' (*Berufsethik*) were not first products of the Reformation and Lutheran teaching. Every vocation in fact has its own ethic. In the transition from medieval to modern times, he writes,

> Business came to be conceived in vocational form and moved to the forefront of life's interests, so that life's other concerns, while by no means absorbed in it, had to be to a certain extent subordinated and adapted to it. Attention to business became a contant motive, controlling and regulating one's entire

conduct of life. Business would be conducted purposely, reaching its height in the specific virtue of the 'capitalist spirit': speculative calculation, speedy and accurate assessment of the situation and of the necessary means to the goal of entrepreneurial success. This in a nutshell is what Sombart means by 'calculativeness' [*Rechenhaftigkeit*].

(1909:110)

This 'capitalist style' and calculative ethos did not first emerge out of the secularisation of Reformation principles.

Contrary to Weber, Rachfahl asserts that the Calvinists' preoccupation with work and charity rather than profit and riches meant they could never have become true capitalists like Fugger. Calvinism would have only appealed to small businessmen and craftsmen, who are not true capitalists for Rachfahl. In Calvin's Geneva, the subordination of economic life to the religious idea may have at most fostered economic stability; but again this is not capitalism. Calvin regarded worldly riches not as evil in itself but as nonetheless 'thin ice' that could lead to sin. One should have no concern for one's possessions and should give to the poor. Any profit existed to serve the glory of God and the greater good of the community. Cromwell's and Baxter's pronouncements on these matters would have seemed to ordinary people like solemn laws, firmly damming up any incipient capitalist spirit. Therefore, if the capitalist spirit really grew out of Puritanism, the Puritans ought to have recognised this as a distortion of all they stood for:

> There are certain qualities Weber sees in Puritan capitalism such as self-righteous sober lawfulness, a consciousness of irreproachability, a formally hard character, a pharisaical good conscience, and so on. If these were really derived by their carriers from the vocational ethic, or if the vocational ethic were invoked by these people to justify and ground such forms of behaviour, they would have to be seen as distortions and aberrations, as a misprision of the true essence of Reformed morality. The Reformation would have had every reason to reject the spiritual authority of such a 'vocational ethic'.

(1909:113)

Finally, Rachfahl argues for a variety of alternative political reasons for capitalist development, such as the non-suppression of religious dissent and subordination of church to state in certain countries. Factors to do with landscape, natural resources, points of communication and population were also responsible, especially at cities such as Hamburg and Danzig. Hamburg in particular remained prosperous throughout, despite the supposed restraining influence of Lutheranism. In general, theological teaching was ignored where economic advantage was at stake, or a variety of practical compromises would be made. In countries such as England and Holland, it was the emergent culture of tolerance and individualism that drove commercial life forward, with the legacy of Erasmus and Renaissance humanism playing a leading role in Holland; whereas Catholic countries such as Austria and Spain had to wait for the eighteenth-century Enlightenment before confessional obsessions were dispelled and capitalist development could begin. Although Calvinism itself later issued in a spirit of individualism and rationalism, its methods of church discipline were at first extremely authoritarian. In Rachfahl's words,

> It was a tragic necessity that a child of individualism and freedom of conscience such as Protestantism had forcibly to suppress these values at first in order to make them possible for later times. Had it tolerated them in its beginnings, it would never have prevailed.
>
> (1909:129)

What was decisive for commercial growth in England after the Civil War was tolerance of sectarian groupings in alliance with rising calls for popular sovereignty. All this, however, was anathema to the original Calvinist theocracy which spurned political equality as contrary to God's hierarchy and rigidly sought to enforce conformity to church law.

In conclusion, Rachfahl views the action of religious factors on economic life at best in a negative fashion. In the absence of traditional restraints on capitalism, such as Catholic asceticism, religion would not hinder economic development; but it could never positively encourage it. Calvinism might act as a useful prick of conscience, pharisaically reassuring and legitimating those already established in wealth and business; but, in general, the whole tenor of Calvinist doctrine opposed worldly riches, and this could have seldom attracted any true capitalist.

CHAPTER 6

Weber's First Reply to Felix Rachfahl, 1910

From the *Archiv für Sozialwissenschaft und Sozialpolitik*, vol. 30, pp. 176–202

In the *Internationale Wochenschrift* (vol. 3, 1909, nos. 39–43) Professor Rachfahl published a critique of my essays on the Protestant ethic and the 'spirit' of capitalism (see my article in *Christliche Welt*, 1906, and earlier Replies to Karl Fischer, *Archiv*, XXV and XXVI).[i] [i] As this critique is also directed (secondarily) at my friend Ernst Troeltsch, he will reply in the same publication.[ii] Although it would have been most natural and useful for me to reply there too, I unfortunately felt (and still feel) unable to do so, despite my regard for its editor, whose leadership of the *Deutsche Literaturzeitung* I also respect. Founded by F. Althoff,[iii] the *Internationale Wochenschrift* has certain editorial practices to which I do not feel inclined to adapt myself. I could of course have ignored these practices as my concern here is merely with polemic. However, the editors have preferred to approach *solely* my colleague Troeltsch, despite the article's being almost entirely directed at *me*. I would of course have ignored this impoliteness, if it were not for the fact that my critic treats both of us as one, in order to make each of us responsible for the other, allowing him to make actual or supposed errors on the part of one of us apply to the other. And nor has he refrained from playing us off against each other so as to make this 'Weber–Troeltsch collective' appear in contradiction with itself. In view of this not very honourable practice, I have decided to go my own way and expressly deny all responsibility for anything not said by *me*, as Troeltsch would undoubtedly do too.

---

[i]   Article in *Christliche Welt*: Weber 1906b.
[ii]   Rachfahl discusses Troeltsch 1906a and 1906b.
[iii]   Friedrich Althoff (1839–1908): Prussian state official and minister of education, founder of the University of Strasbourg in 1871 and professor of law there until 1882.

The Protestant Ethic Debate

I might also be permitted to add the following. Anyone who has genuinely read both our essays will know that Troeltsch does not need *my* results *at all* for *his* purposes and positions – except for the concept of the *sects*, which Rachfahl does not even mention (see *Archiv*, XXI:63f./PE:144f., and my article in *Christliche Welt*). His findings could be right even if mine were wrong, and vice versa. He explores the historical development of the *social teachings* of the Christian churches, whereas I have so far only tried to clarify a particular phenomenon of *conduct of life* in its (original) religious conditioning. If he occasionally referred to works of mine,[2] it was always a case of areas peripheral to his concerns (except in the case not at issue here concerning church and sects). And let me also stress here that no collaboration at all, not even latent collaboration, took place in this. My work on these issues was not first set in train by Sombart's book on capitalism, as Rachfahl assumes, relying on Troeltsch. I lectured on them in part as much as 12 years ago [1897] (see my explicit comments at *Archiv* (XX:19, n.1/PE:198, n.14).[iv] Troeltsch has been pursuing his own themes for a long time along very much his own paths. It may well be that he was prompted to reflect on his problems from economic–sociological points of view by individual remarks in my essay and by other writers, as he has occasionally said. But this is by no means one party's 'adoption' of the other's 'theory', simply the objective *fact* that everyone who once sees these connections must arrive at a similar viewpoint. This is what accounts for my writings seeming to *fill out* Troeltsch's much wider field. If I had continued my essay, I too would have needed to deal with large areas of the ground now covered by Troeltsch. As a non-theologian, I would never have been able to accomplish this in the same way as Troeltsch. But as far as my own earlier studies allow me to judge, I see no points at all important on which to contradict his account. Least of all can I extract any such points from the trivialities Rachfahl raises against him. However, Troeltsch will of course have to take scientific *responsibility* alone for what he has said, just as I will for my remarks. I have commented on Troeltsch's article here only in order that critics like Rachfahl do not read into this separation of responsibilities a *rejection* of Troeltsch's findings on my part. Now to the matter at hand.

Rachfahl's polemic starts to go wrong from the very first word in the title of his piece: '*Calvinism* and capitalism'. From the first moment I mention Calvinism in my essay (contrasting it with Catholicism and Lutheranism) (XX:10, 50, 52/PE:43, 87, 88), I speak of its importance as entirely equal to that of those *sects* (or sect-like groupings within the church) which I generically called '*ascetic*

[iv] At *Archiv* (XX:19, n.1/PE:198, n.14) Weber acknowledges the significance of Sombart (1902) but also states that 'the following studies go back in their most important points of view to much older work' of Weber's own.

Protestantism' in the title of my second chapter and throughout.³ To get this clear from the start, Rachfahl now inveighs in the most wide-ranging way possible against the *name* 'asceticism' for the kind of conduct of life I sought to analyse. And this is actually the only thing from his strange 'critique' *he himself* still upholds unreservedly by the end – despite the fact that he could not avoid using this expression for the same thing at the beginning of his article.⁴ But, as we shall see, this recurrent discrepancy between the yardsticks he uses for himself and those he uses for others never bothers him – and, of course, there is still always a difference between the view of a historical 'specialist' and the view of an outsider who merely 'contrives' history, even when they say the same thing!

According to Rachfahl, asceticism is 'flight from the world'. Therefore, because the Puritans (including all 'ascetic' sects) were not monks or similarly contemplative beings, what I call '*inner-worldly* asceticism' is in fact a 'false' concept that erroneously presupposes an affinity with Catholic asceticism. I can hardly think of a more sterile polemic than one about *names*. As far as I am concerned, the *name* can be changed for any other that fits better. If we are not to coin completely new words each time or invent symbols, like chemists or like the philosopher Avenarius,ᵛ we must give every phenomenon to which no term has yet been accorded the nearest and most descriptive words from traditional language and just be careful to *define* them unambiguously – as I believe I have done quite sufficiently with '*inner-worldly* asceticism'.⁵

As far as any inner affinity with Catholic asceticism is concerned, let me remind the reader that when Ritschlᵛⁱ went so far in identifying certain ascetic (in *my* sense) features of 'Pietism' (broadly understood in his work) with 'Catholic' traces in Protestantism, I tried to *restrict* his account. And when even a contemporary of the Reformation such as Sebastian Franckᵛⁱⁱ (whom Troeltsch rightly quotes) saw one of its achievements as being that henceforth not only those called to monastic orders but *every single person* had to be a kind of life-long monk, he meant exactly the same as me. Nonetheless, if Rachfahl is to be believed, both

---

ᵛ   Richard Avenarius (1843–96): a naturalistic philosopher of the late nineteenth century who coined the term 'empirio-criticism', the object of Lenin's polemical treatise *Materialism and Empirio-Criticism*, 1908.

ᵛⁱ   Albrecht Ritschl (1822–89): influential Protestant theologian based at Göttingen, author of *The Christian Doctrine of Justification and Reconciliation* (1870–74) and *Geschichte des Pietismus* [*History of Pietism*] (1880–86). Ritschl and his school's eminently social–ethical understanding of salvation and the Kingdom of God was an important influence on the meetings of the Social–Evangelical Congress in the 1890s and the weekly journal *Christliche Welt* (founded in 1887), as well as on Troeltsch and numerous other contemporary theologians and social critics.

ᵛⁱⁱ Sebastian Franck (1499–1542): prominent Lutheran minister who became a member of the Anabaptists in 1528. Note Weber's citation of him in the second edition of *The Protestant Ethic* (PE:121).

Franck and I deserve to be gravely reminded that a monk is not allowed a wife, to earn money, or to become at all attached to the things of this world, and that the expression is therefore most unsuitable. Yet when speaking of 'asceticism' *today*, whether in the specific area of sexuality or general 'pleasures of life', or whether in respect of our attitude to aesthetic or other non-'ethical' values, everyone knows that what we mean is essentially just that kind of conduct of life Puritanism made into a duty (and this includes *not* only Calvinism but the Baptist movement and other groupings as well). Thus this 'asceticism' was an ideal of life – with the difference that it had to be exercised *within* the world-orders of family, earning a living and community life, and its material demands had to be modified accordingly. In its 'spirit', it was an ideal common to both the Protestant movements and to those *rational* forms of *methodical* life regulation [*Lebensmethodik*] that governed monastic asceticism. I explained this for various spheres of life, including some lying outside the sphere of 'acquisition' – in brief outline, but still clearly enough not to need to repeat myself here.[6] Even the *means* by which Protestant asceticism operates run quite parallel to those of the earlier asceticism, as I remarked (XXI:77ff./PE:157ff.).[viii] I also pointed out that it was precisely the monasteries' asceticism that made them capable of such great economic achievements. I could have added that, with their peculiarly bourgeois behaviour, the rational–ascetic sects or sect-like groupings of the Middle Ages very regularly evinced quite similar characteristics to those of the Baptist sects later and the corresponding Russian sects (though not all them!). But that '*the* early Protestantism' *as a whole* 'took over' asceticism 'from medieval Catholicism' is one of numerous stupid claims Rachfahl imputes to me. It can be seen fully in my work how keenly and ruthlessly those characteristics I analysed were attacked as 'work holiness' (*Werkheiligkeit*) by the Lutheran, Anglican and otherwise *non*-'ascetic' (in my sense) flank of early Protestantism – just as these denominations attacked Catholic monasticism. So Protestantism was very far from united in its attitude to asceticism (in my sense). Yet for now, I know no better word than 'ascetic' to characterise *generically* the groups I was dealing with, in contrast to Lutheranism, Anglicanism, and the more diluted varieties of the Reformed church. These 'ascetic' groups *did* share *common* differences from the other Protestant movements, even though the direction in which they developed was *just* as much a product of the events known collectively as the 'Reformation' as,

---

[viii] Weber mentions two things in particular here: labour and sexual abstinence. Labour, he comments, is 'an approved ascetic technique, as it has always been in the Western Church', while 'the sexual asceticism of Puritanism differs only in degree, not in fundamental principle, from that of monasticism' (XXI:79/PE:158).

for example, the Gnesio-Lutherans.[ix] And incidentally – God knows – the 'spirit' of this last grouping was scarcely any less different from that of Luther in the 1520s than was the 'Calvinism' that interests me from the personal views of Calvin himself – *as I myself emphatically stressed* (XXI:6, n.5/PE:220, n.7) yet now find didactically levelled back at me.

But what kind of 'historian' hurls *value-judgements* such as 'distortion' at a phenomenon such as the Puritan ethic of acquisition (and note: at the phenomenon *itself*, not my account of it) just because it does not fit into the conceptual scheme he has made for himself? Just because it is non-'ethical' and *antipathic* despite being of enormous consequence, as he himself admits? Just because it does not fit into the Protestant ethic's course as he feels it really *should* have been?[7] What kind of methodologist puts forward the strange thesis that in England the existence of the capitalist spirit 'would also be *understandable* without this' (religious) 'element', even though he '*by no means* wishes to deny its influence'? So he means an 'element' that is causally important for a certain constellation, yet one he feels the 'historian' can *nevertheless* leave aside as irrelevant to his 'understanding' of that constellation. We might as well substitute 'fabricate' for 'understand' here, since, despite his disciplinary patriotism [*ressortpatriotischen Eifer*] against untrained 'fabricators of history', Rachfahl clearly represents an ideal-type of those confusions that frequently befall historians whenever they blindly employ *unexplained concepts* riddled with prejudices and value-judgements.

There is no certified concept of 'asceticism'.[8] Fairly obviously, it is possible to understand the concept much more widely than when I compared the kind of conduct of life I termed '*inner-worldly* asceticism' with monastic 'otherworldly' asceticism; and I have acknowledged this myself. In speaking of Catholic asceticism, I *specifically* mean *rationalised* asceticism (shown most powerfully by the Jesuit order) in *contrast* to 'unsystematic flight from the world' on the Catholic side and merely emotional 'asceticism' (*bloße Gefühls-'Askese'*) on the Protestant side. My concept therefore emphatically *diverges* from Troeltsch's, as anyone with any goodwill must see – even Rachfahl. And he *did* 'see' it – he even speaks of '*fundamental*' oppositions between our two views.[9] But *nevertheless*, where it happens to suit him, he struggles on with a 'Troeltsch–Weber' concept of asceticism; and in order to 'refute' it, he collects all kinds of concepts of 'asceticism' from other writers, which may be suitable for *their* purposes but not for mine. I also explain fully at the start of my discussion (XX:35/PE:78), and emphasise again later for

---

[ix] The Gnesio-Lutherans, or 'Genuine Lutherans', were a grouping within Lutheranism prominent until the 1570s based at Jena who opposed the more humanistic teachings of the Philippian Lutherans centred at Wittenberg who followed the theology of Melanchthon.

good measure (*Archiv*, XXVI:278, n.2),[x] that one can engage in 'rationalisation' of life from very different viewpoints, and therefore that one can understand very different things by 'rationalisation.' Yet Rachfahl still wants to use this remark as an 'objection' to me – even though here again, everything I understand by asceticism for *my* purposes I stated clearly enough, as he well knows. I confess I consider a discussion like this fairly worthless and hard to stomach when a writer who so thrives on deliberate and artificial confusion over *words* fears that my clearly ad hoc but nonetheless definite use of language [*mein bestimmter, deutlich ad hoc geschaffener Sprachgebrauch*] might 'blur fundamental distinctions'. Supposing we were to try to rescue something positive from Rachfahl's case, where in *his* writing would we find 'fundamental' distinctions?

But let us return to the beginning. Rachfahl's quite arbitrary restriction of the subject to 'Calvinism' sets the tone for almost his whole argument against me.[10] Straight away he makes this the real theme of his polemic, and constantly twists the discussion back to it. This is the only thing that allows him to sustain his single serious thesis against me.

Let me deal with this thesis straight away. Rachfahl is convinced of the key role of 'tolerance' in economic development. Now, as every reader of my essay knows, I do not differ with him here at all; I too have mentioned this, albeit not in any great detail so far (XXI:42, n.1/PE:242, n.110). Certainly in the circumstances of the time, any kind of tolerance was bound to contribute 'to populating the country', to importing *wealth* and trade from abroad – but *this* aspect is not what interests me. For me, what was decisive, with regard to the development of that *habitus* I christened 'capitalist spirit' (ad hoc and just for my own purposes), was clearly *who in actual cases benefited from tolerance*. If those who benefited were, for example, the Jews or the 'ascetic' Christian denominations (in my sense of 'ascetic') (XXI:28f./PE:118f.), then 'tolerance' regularly worked to disseminate this 'spirit' – but of course we cannot see this dissemination simply as a result of 'tolerance' on its own. And in particular, the *degree* of 'tolerance' was generally far from decisive for the degree of development of 'capitalist spirit' (still in my sense). For we know that, conversely, *incomplete* tolerance, i.e. systematic exclusion of minority religious groups from equal rights in state and society, often served to drive *déclassé* elements onto the path of economic acquisition particularly powerfully (see XX:5/PE:39). This explains why those who *most* seem to have been affected by this were the 'churches under the cross'.[xi] Indeed this is what Sir William Petty emphasised – whom Rachfahl quotes – when he remarked that everywhere 'business' lay in the hands of the heterodox, and that in countries dominated by the

---

[x] Second Reply to Karl Fischer, 1908, n.2 (see p.49, in this volume).
[xi] Another name for the persecuted churches, sects and heretical movements.

Roman church 'three-quarters' of all business lay in heretic hands.[xii] But now we come to the *fact* – the really significant point I stressed from the outset (XX:6/PE:38f.) – that disenfranchised or disadvantaged *Catholic* minorities *never, right until today,* demonstrated this prominence in business at all obviously.[11] Nor have even the Lutheran minorities ever demonstrated it like the 'ascetic' denominations. By contrast, Calvinist, Quaker and Baptist groups tend to display these cultural and economic characteristics both when they are in a minority and when they are *dominant*; and wherever these 'ascetic' Protestant denominations compete equally with other Christian denominations, they have regularly been the dominant vehicle of economic life. In the classic old industrial area of the Wupper valley, even in the last generation, members of the 'Reformed' church led their lives in a radically different way from those of the old church; and these differences lay *precisely in the decisive characteristics discussed here.* The business activity of the 'vocational people' ('*Berufsmenschen*') that flowed from what I purposely called their 'ascetic compulsion to save' (*asketischer Sparzwang*) was strikingly apparent in Reformed and Pietistic circles (Pietism is Reformed in provenance) – despite all Rachfahl's fictitious 'common Christian morality' (*gemeinchristliche Sittlichkeit*). Anyone who has lived there will confirm this. Their whole way of life so closely matched my description – incomplete as it doubtless was – that several different members of these circles assured me directly that only now, and only by reference to these antecedents, did they fully understand the uniqueness of their own traditions. And if Rachfahl holds up Lutheran Hamburg as an example of a place where the 'capitalist spirit' flourished and still flourishes *without* the assistance of 'ascetic' Protestant influences, I can content myself for now by drawing on a friendly letter from my colleague Adalbert Wahl in Hamburg.[xiii] According to this letter, in characteristic contrast to the situation its author knew in Reformed Basle where the old patriciate thriftily hold on to their wealth, *none* of the now considerable family fortunes in Hamburg, including those counted as old inherited ones, date back to the seventeenth century – with just *one* exception, and this is the case of a well-known family of the Reformed [i.e. Calvinist, not Lutheran] church.

But enough of such details. If I wanted, I could have mentioned further personal communications on the activities of the Baptists and others. All I want to underline here is that my key 'thesis' about the significance of the 'calling' offered something 'new' only in the manner of its elaboration. On the matter at hand, I still agree with what that outstanding contemporary, Sir William Petty – whom

---

[xii] William Petty, *Political Arithmetick, or a Discourse Concerning the Extent and Value of Lands, People, Buildings, etc.*, London: Robert Clavel, 1691, p.26.
[xiii] Adalbert Wahl: professor of history at Hamburg, b. 1871.

Rachfahl well knows and recognises as an authority since he thinks he can use Petty's remarks about the economic blessings of tolerance *against* me, albeit manifestly in a contorted way – said just *two pages earlier* [in the text already cited] about the reasons for tolerance having such a favourable effect on 'business', especially in Holland: 'I now come to the first policy of the Dutch, viz.: liberty of Conscience ... Dissenters of this kind' – he means the supporters of the Dutch struggle for freedom, primarily Calvinists – 'are for the most part thinking, sober and patient Men, and such as believe *that Labour and Industry is their Duty towards God* (How erroneous soever their Opinions be).'[12][xiv] The passage almost seems to make one of the basic theses of my essay an unfortunate unconscious *plagiarism* of Petty – so much so that I could leave the reader to choose between Petty's authority and modern critics, and myself bow out of the discussion.[13] I would do so all the more willingly as I have to confess that Groen van Prinsterer[xv] – who can, after all, be trusted to give a substantially more thorough and original analysis of his native land than Rachfahl, whatever else one may credit him for – said essentially the same about the generation of wealth in Holland, with reference to the relatively low proportion of expenditure to income.[14]

Petty's passage then goes on to clarify a further point which Rachfahl makes into another of his spurious controversies and lets dominate his essay almost throughout:

> These People [Puritan Dissenters] believing the Justice of God, and seeing the most Licentious persons to enjoy most of the World, and its best things, will never venture to be of the same Religion and Profession with Voluptuaries and Men of extreme Wealth and Power, who they think have their Portion in this World.[xvi]

So, it was *not* the great concessionaires and monopolists, the economic 'supermen' found in *all* ages of commercial or colonial expansion, but their *opponents*, the much broader strata of bourgeois *rising middle estates* (*bürgerliche aufsteigende Mittelstände*), who were the typical vehicle of the Puritan world-view – as I stressed myself most emphatically. But even though Rachfahl knows this (because he quotes it), he still makes it an objection to me, as always whenever it suits him.[15] Taken together, Petty's remarks clearly mean to illustrate Protestant

---

[xiv] Ibid. p.23.

[xv] Guillaume Groen van Prinsterer (1801–76): Dutch Calvinist political leader, historian and religious thinker, author of a handbook of Dutch history (1846) outlining his view of the providential genesis of the Dutch republic and *Ongeloof en Revolutie* ('Unbelief and Revolution') (1847). Groen became one of the pillars of the Reveil, a conservative religious revivalist movement that paved the way for Abraham Kuyper's Anti-Revolutionary Party, formed in 1878.

[xvi] Ibid. pp.23–24. 'Puritan Dissenters' is Weber's addition.

asceticism's (apparently!) paradoxical attitude to wealth (in my sense of 'asceticism'). This entirely corresponds to what I gathered from other sources and especially from the principles of ascetic denominations up until their weakened forms today. As the source of the lust for pleasure and power, wealth as such is not just *a* but *the* danger. Desire for worldly goods is in itself absolutely reprehensible (I could quote as many passages as I wished). This too is what Petty means. And yet speaking of these people who were so *hostile* to wealth and the rich, Petty himself spoke precisely of their 'industry' as a particularly important source of wealth-creation and underlined their overwhelming contribution to enterprise – again, just as I do. How easily this apparent paradox can be resolved will be appreciated by anyone who has genuinely read my essays. Rachfahl knows this too, even if the way he paraphrases me on this score is more than a little strange.[16] For he is well-acquainted with my detailed comments on that curious attitude of the Puritans toward acquiring goods, so hard for us to imagine today without a suspicion of hypocrisy and self-deception but by no means so 'complicated' for those people who had to find a bridge between this world and the next. Moreover, Rachfahl knows the explicit *distinction* I drew between this and the habitus expressed in the remark Sombart quotes from Fugger (XX:15/PE:51).[xvii] And he knows my express reminder that the whole *type* of person represented by the big Italian, German, English, Dutch and overseas financiers is a type *known throughout history* and *in no way* characteristic of the 'early capitalism' of modern times, as I am forced to repeat yet again.[17] It crucially differs from those aspects of early capitalism I sought to reveal that so easily escape notice yet are among the most important. Rachfahl's close acquaintance with my views has still not prevented him trying to counter me with that type of capitalist who *lacks* the trait I call 'ascetic', even though he should know that this type has been around since the Pharaohs' time. He asks me whether *this* type might not represent the 'true' capitalist spirit, even though I state with the greatest clarity that these are not the men I am concerned with. I am *not*, for example, concerned with that well-known type of 'acquisitive' trader in Holland who 'would go through hell for gain, even though he scorched his sails' (*and note that I quoted these words myself in my essay*) (XX:20/PE:57).[18] *Readers* of my essay will surely see that I owe no answer to Rachfahl here. It is the same when he eagerly sniffs out all kinds of regions with strongly developed capitalist economies in which 'Protestant asceticism' played no (actual or alleged) decisive role, or conversely in which Protestant asceticism did manifest itself but

---

xvii This is once again Weber's distinction between Fugger's wanting 'to make money as long as he could' and Franklin's 'time is money': 'What in the former case was an expression of commercial daring and a personal inclination morally neutral, in the latter takes on the character of an ethically coloured maxim for the conduct of life' (XX:15/PE:51f.).

no large-scale capitalist economies developed as a result. I have discussed the details of these criticisms already, indeed repeatedly and sufficiently. However, I have no objection to going over them again, for it may just be that we have arrived at a point where debate between our two standpoints seems possible?

I said only *'seems'*, however. For, unfortunately, Rachfahl actually has no viewpoint of his own that could be debated with *at all*. He leaves us only sand to chew over.[xviii] One wonders in vain at the point of his five-part tirade against me when he finally declares that the religious moments I discussed will 'certainly have to be acknowledged as having great significance for economic development' – although, he continues, 'not exactly in the same direction' I had described; or at least, as he immediately concedes, *if* in that direction, then not so exclusively as I had argued (*where* he refers to here I know not). But then, he goes on: 'the vocational ethic of the Reformation' was *'undoubtedly'* one of the elements that fostered economic development, was even (he says shortly afterward) one of the 'driving forces'. He even claims (mistakenly) that I analysed this aspect of its significance first in my essay, and the only reservation he manages to sustain concerns my *description* of the ethic as 'ascetic'. I thank my censor for conceding me these points. After all, I myself stressed emphatically that I had no intention of assuming anything *more* than just the existence of this 'driving force'.

To what extent this force, relative to other factors, actually influenced matters in the direction appropriate to it[xix] I have not tried to determine 'in detail' (as Rachfahl wishes), however important a task this certainly is. This can only be tackled for individual countries separately and is not easy.[19] Rachfahl's expectation that I employ statistics here I consider altogether innocuous, as must anyone who knows from experience what enormous difficulties pile up against the attempt to *measure* the motivational influence of a particular world-view that is undoubtedly still with us today.[20] *My* chosen task – laid out as clearly as possible in my essay – was first and foremost to establish not where and how strongly but *how*, through what psychological structures of motivation, particular forms of Protestant belief came to exert the effects they did – as even Rahfahl agrees they did. *That* they had this influence I of course at first *illustrated* with a number of examples, but otherwise I assumed this to be generally known – because I was by no means saying anything 'new' here. Even Rachfahl explicitly assumes this to be

---

[xviii] *'Man kaut bei ihm auf Sand.'* Possibly a pun on *kauen* (chew over, think over) and *bauen* (build, building on sand).

[xix] What Weber means by this phrase (*In welchem Maße sie … faktisch in der ihr adäquaten Richtung gewirkt hat*) is not entirely clear; but, drawing on his ideal–typical method, he might mean the extent to which, in actual historical cases, religious determinants of action approximated to an ideal-type of purely religiously determined action (as distinct from action determined by material–economic or other factors).

incontestable and 'beyond doubt',[21] although his next sentence, in which he says that we must now prove these connections exist, sounds strange enough (and I suspect not just to the non-historian!).[22] Rachfahl then declares that I made *this* 'task' 'light' for myself – though I said I had not set it myself. I must wait and see whether other readers have the impression that I took the work I *really* had in mind too 'lightly'. But in view of such truly presumptuous remarks, one wonders how 'difficult' the demanding critic has made the task I have 'not carried out'. Given that in all five sections of his essay nothing, *absolutely nothing* (or tell me what!) is advanced which was not already in my text about the relationship even between Calvinism (which is all that Rachfahl talks about) and capitalism, I might have refrained from replying. There is really nothing else I can do except simply request those interested to look at my essay again *after* Rachfahl's 'critique' and read it *in its entirety* – demanding and immodest as this request may be. Then they will find the following:

1 Not only did I *myself* call it 'foolish' to imply that it would be possible to derive the capitalist *economic system* from religious motives in general or from the work ethic of what I called 'ascetic' Protestantism. At the same time, I emphasised in the greatest detail, and in fact by way of *showing the reasons* for my approach to the problem, that 'capitalist spirit' has existed *without* any capitalist *economy* (Franklin) *just as much* as the other way round (all of which Rachfahl himself quotes, but forgets again as soon as it suits him and then raises as an 'objection' to me).[23]

2 It did not occur to me to *identify* those motives I believed were originally religiously determined and 'of ascetic character' with the capitalist spirit (as Rachfahl lets his readers assume from beginning to end – even in his résumé). I portray them only as *one* constitutive element *among others* of this 'spirit' (and constitutive of *other* features of modern culture as well!) (XXI:107/PE:180). As I said, after endless prevarication, Rachfahl finally admits this to be correct.

3 I have described the relation of the so-called *'acquisitive drive'* ['*Erwerbstrieb*'] to the 'capitalist spirit' so unambiguously that Rachfahl's remarks on this issue are just further evidence *either* that he is *not* inclined to polemicise with sufficient goodwill to assume *any* reasonable meaning in his opponent's statements (I will not even say *possible* reasonable meaning) *or* that when writing his 'critique' he forgot what was said in the work criticised.

We will leave aside the question of whether the standard expression 'acquisitive drive' should be used at all for the highly heterogeneous kinds of mentality that can underlie the striving for money and possessions. This term stems from an otherwise long-outmoded school of psychology, but probably cannot be dispensed with altogether. One of the most explicit premises of my account is that this so-called 'drive' has existed on a colossal scale in precisely a *compulsive*, irrational, unbridled form at all stages of cultural development and in all possible social strata: in the Neapolitan *barcaiuolo*,[xx] the ancient and modern oriental shopkeeper, the 'worthy' Tyrolean landlord, the 'long-suffering' farmer, the African chieftain; but *not* in such a naively compulsive form in the 'typical' Puritan or in such a strictly 'upright' man as Benjamin Franklin. I might have expected that this, at least, would not escape someone who sought to 'criticise' my account. And, to repeat *yet* again, wherever large-scale capitalist development has taken place, in distant antiquity as well as our own day, unscrupulous money-makers[xxi] have always existed, whether in the exploitation of the Roman provinces or in the robber colonies of the Italian coastal towns or the worldwide speculations of the Florentine 'financiers', the slave-owner plantations, the goldfields of all continents, the American railways, the grand princes of the Far East, or the equally worldwide speculations of London City 'imperialists'. The differences here lie in technological means and opportunities, *not* in the *psychology* of acquisition. I think Rachfahl could have spared himself such astounding revelations as that the striving for 'happiness', 'advantage', 'pleasure', 'honour', 'power', 'the future of one's descendants' and such like were and are always and everywhere involved in very different combinations in triggering the striving for the greatest possible profit – it will be difficult to find anyone to dispute this.[24] I mentioned these motives only and *specifically* where *tension* arose between their influence and the ascetic 'ethic of the calling' that interests me (XXI:98, n.65/PE:276, n.79).

Equally astonishingly, Rachfahl is also correct to argue that there are transitional psychological states between all the other various kinds of inner orientation towards acquisition and the one that concerned me, and further that the motive I *portrayed*[25] 'in isolation' 'cannot be completely isolated' in reality and is mostly 'combined with others' and is not exhaustive 'even today', and so on.[26] This, however, could be true of any motive of human action, and has so far stopped no one from analysing the *specific* effects of a particular motive and seeking the greatest 'isolation' and inner consistency as possible. Anyone not interested in this whole 'psychology' but only in the external forms of economic *systems* I would ask to leave my efforts unread. They can then kindly leave it to *me* whether I should interest myself in this psychological aspect of modern economic development revealed by Puritanism – revealed in its unique balancing of great inner tensions and conflicts between 'calling', 'ethos' and 'life' (as we like to say today). No such balance of forces existed either before or since then. Where

---

[xx]   Boatmen, ferrymen.
[xxi] English in original.

ancient and medieval traditions pointed to other routes, we today are experiencing renewed tensions which reach far beyond the sphere of activity I originally singled out and are turning into cultural problems of the first order that only our 'bourgeois' world knows.

It is simply untrue when Rachfahl claims out of the blue that the 'vocational ethic' known to 'ascetic' Protestantism (in my sense) prevailed in the Middle Ages as well. (And as with all his polemic, this claim stands in glaring contradiction to his concessions at the end.) His more peripheral points about church doctrine on 'usury' in the Middle Ages are not at all decisive for me, as every reader of my essay should know. Indeed, his remarks on this subject are classic witnesses to his complete misunderstanding of the problem. To quote him:

> And if a capitalist really felt so bothered by it [the ban on interest] that he had to *appease* his conscience through pious endowments – is that not evidence that his *fundamental outlook* was anti-traditionalist? The *acquisitive drive* was so powerful in him *that he did not even need the vehicle of religious ethics to feel driven to make money like the Protestant 'ascetics' later.*[27]

What about the 'acquisitive drive' of all those company founders and speculators who 'brush their sleeves against the prison walls' in order to make millions,[xxii] or the 'acquisitive drive' of the waiter schooled to shamelessness in the tourist Riviera who habitually swindles his guests? Such people need the 'vehicle' of an 'ethics' even less. If a scale for measuring 'acquisitive *drive*' were constructed, Puritanism would certainly not come top, and nor would that type of acquisitive rationalist I saw in Franklin.[28] But it is not a matter of compulsive greed for money, happiness or family glory: all such things lay further from the minds of *serious* Puritans than from other groups; for they became rich *in spite of* their rejection of the world. The point is that 'ascetic' Protestantism has created for capitalism a corresponding 'soul', the soul of the 'man with a calling' who *does not need* the same means of feeling at one with his actions as the man of the Middle Ages. The merchant of the Florentine early Renaissance did not feel at one with his actions. Here is not the place to analyse the deep inner conflict running through the most serious men of those days, despite all their overflowing energy and apparent inner unity. These men's restitution of property gained 'usuriously' is just one phenomenon that fits this picture, and certainly a rather superficial one. But fit this picture it certainly does. I – and indeed anyone at all impartial – can only see in such 'means of self-appeasement' [*Beschwichtigungsmitteln*] one of the many symptoms of *tension* between 'conscience' and 'action', of the incompatibility of the ideals

---

[xxii] Weber means businessmen who tread a fine line between the legal and the illegal, or 'rub shoulders with the law'.

of the *serious*-minded Catholic and the 'Deo placere non potest' with 'mercantile' striving for profit – an incompatibility unsurmounted even by Luther. One can understand those men's countless practical and theoretical 'compromises' precisely as 'compromises'.[29] It is simply untrue that all occupations have always generated their own 'vocational ethic' in just the same way – as Rachfahl maintains and seems so 'obvious'. Clearly no one, least of all I, disputes the trivial correctness of this (in essence historical–materialist) theory, but one purpose of my essay could have been to establish its *limitations*.[30]

To sum up: my explanations sought to analyse a particular constitutive component of the *lifestyle* that stood at the cradle of modern capitalism which – along with numerous other forces – it helped set in motion, and to trace its transformations and desuetude. Such a project cannot determine what has existed wherever and *whenever* capitalism has existed; it has to do the reverse and determine the *specificity* of a unique development.[31] I have already sharply refused responsibility for others considering as absolute the religious factors I *expressly* described as *single components* and identifying them with the 'spirit' of capitalism *in general* or even *deriving* capitalism from them. Even though Rachfahl knows this, he felt no duty to take notice. My attempt may have succeeded or failed. But if a historian does not know how to counter it any better than listing a series of *other* components which have *always* accompanied periods of capitalist expansion – as no one doubts – he does little to serve the purposes and interests of his discipline. Why take an interest in 'history' if all this establishes is that basically 'all's been said before'?

Enough. Now just a few more remarks about the relationship of the 'spirit' of capitalism to capitalism as an economic *system*.

Werner Sombart has made a study of this subject (*Archiv*, XXIX:689ff.),[xxiii] which in its broad agreement on all significant points, especially methodological, relieves me of the obligation to go into detail.[32] Both the concepts of 'capitalism', and even more so, 'spirit of capitalism', can only be construed as 'ideal–typical' constructs of thought.[33] Indeed both can be construed either *abstractly*, such that what is *permanently* similar is distilled out in conceptual purity; in which case the second concept becomes rather empty and almost purely a function of the first. Or they can be construed *historically*, such that, for one particular epoch in *contrast* to others, 'ideal–typical' mental pictures are formed of *specific* features that are presumed to be *generally* present and therefore likewise given and known about. Then of course it is a question of features not so present in other epochs to which the construct is applied, or else present in a specifically *different* degree. This is what I tried to do for the 'capitalism' of the ancient world as an economic *system*, although certainly in a very incomplete way (see my 'Agrarverhältnisse im

---

Altertum', in *Handwörterbuch der Staatwissenschaft*, third edition, vol. 1, 1909).[34][xxiv] For what I chose to call the '*spirit*' of *modern* capitalism, my essay was meant to be the *beginning*[35] of an exposition that sought first of all to trace the new threads woven into capitalist development during the Reformation period.

Now to the question of what we can understand by the 'spirit' of capitalism in relation to 'capitalism' itself. As far as 'capitalism' *itself* is concerned, this can only mean a particular 'economic *system*', i.e. a form of 'economic' behaviour towards people and material goods involving 'investment' of 'capital', whose modus operandi we analyse 'pragmatically' by ascertaining the 'unavoidable' or 'best' *means* [of action] corresponding to a given type of situation. Again, it must comprise either everything common to such economic systems at all times, or the special characteristics of a particular historical system of this kind. Here we are concerned only with the latter case. A given historical form of 'capitalism' can be fulfilled by very different kinds of 'spirit'; but it can also – and most often will – stand in various graded 'relations of elective affinity' [*Wahlverwandtschaftsverhält-nisse*] to certain historical types of 'spirit'. The 'spirit' can be more or less (or not at all) 'adequate' to the 'form'. There can be no doubt that the *degree* of this adequacy has influenced historical development, and likewise that 'form' and 'spirit' strive to resemble each other, as I said at the time; and finally that where a system and 'spirit' converge with an especially high 'degree of adequacy' to each other, a seamless unitary development sets in of the kind I began to analyse.

Because this crucial concept of the 'spirit' of capitalism (in my case: of modern capitalism)[36] describes an extremely complex historical formation, anything like a *definition* is not possible at the start but only at the conclusion of an investigation as the result of a step-by-step synthesis – as I myself stressed at the beginning of my essay. This applies to all essentially 'historical' concepts. Initially, all one can offer is some graphic means of *illustration*; I therefore took as an example someone from a semi-barter economic milieu, or, at any rate, from a (relatively!) very *un*capitalist milieu: Benjamin Franklin. This was expressly to show the *independence* of the capitalist 'spirit' from the capitalist 'economic system' adequate to it. Earlier, I reminded the reader in an illustrative manner that the 'spirit' is not without influence on the unfolding of the 'economic system', and *explicitly* postponed discussion of the converse causal relationship until the continuation of my essay, which I explicitly described as unfinished. For reasons I clearly stated (originally as well as here) and which since then have only gained in force, the essay has not yet reached its 'conclusion', and this, as I said before, is to my continuing disadvantage. Essentially, only a *part* of the historical development of the idea of the 'calling' and its extension to acquisition is portrayed in my essay.

[xxiv] Weber 1909.

I could not, and had no desire to, claim anything more than this. It fell to a 'criticising' historian to try to pre-empt the result of the desired synthesis with a 'definition'. Rachfahl claims that the 'capitalist spirit' – which for him means that driving force that leads a man to make his fortune – consists of a mixture of 'acquisitive drive' with 'still other' motives: 'consideration' of one's 'happiness' and 'benefit' to oneself or others, especially one's family, striving for pleasures, honours, power, a brilliant position for one's descendants, *and so on*. This 'and so on' of course conceals *every other imaginable* motive, especially, for example, charity – to name just one practically very important 'purpose' of 'capital accumulation'. And as, moreover, he does not know how to distinguish the (subjective) 'spirit' of capitalism from the (objective) economic *system* and equates them both with the 'acquisitive drive', he of course overlooks my assessment of *what* the alpha and omega of the 'gospel of miserliness' in Franklin actually is (XX:17/PE:54), just as he ignores what I say (on the same page) about the *contrast* of acquisitiveness with duty in a calling. Then, despite my explicit reservations, he makes the *other* contrast between 'traditionalistic' and 'acquisition' economies the central point of my discussion. If acquisition were simply a matter of acquiring more than one's 'needs', the *pinnacle* of acquisitive humanity would be the insatiable savage, avid for women and treasures and innocent of all rationalistic calculations – whereas the Puritan would stand toward the other end of this continuum. Economic action sustained by the 'spirit of capitalism' (in my sense) is certainly directly contrary to traditionalism – *this* is what I first established – but it is far from being identical with striving for the greatest possible surplus over one's *needs*. So it does indeed form a contrast with 'traditionalistic' economy but not a complete one – especially as it does *not* coincide with capitalist economic *form*, as I specifically said (XX:23/PE:62) and explained with an example (XX:27f./PE:65f.).[xxv] Finally, the specific component of the modern capitalist 'spirit' I analysed, namely 'duty in a calling', and everything that goes with it, is in turn found only in a *particular slice of economic history*. At the same time, it also extends beyond the economic into quite heterogeneous spheres of human action. My discussion expressly and deliberately confined itself to the development of *'people with a calling'* (*'Berufsmenschentum'*) in relation to this capitalist 'spirit'. I can do absolutely nothing if careless readers see fit to ignore this.

These remarks must come to a close. For on this occasion it is not possible to develop particular parts and views of my essay further, such as the significance of

---

[xxv] At *Archiv* (XX:23/PE:62) and (XX:27f./PE:65f.) Weber mentions the fact that Franklin's printing business 'did not differ in form from any handicraft enterprise' of a much older period, while, conversely, numerous banks, export businesses, large retail establishments and putting-out enterprises have been run in a purely traditionalistic spirit, despite being patently capitalistic in form.

the sects. In an important sense, the *sect* represents for the nascent modern age the archetype of those social groupings which today mould 'public opinion', 'cultural values' and 'individualities'. Neither is it opportune to look any closer at the widely branching routes leading from the Puritan lifestyle to present lifestyles.[37] I regret that such a sterile critique, with its sneering tone, its refusal to understand and unpleasant, pompous type of author, has also provoked a sterile response, costing the *Archiv* space. All that is said *here* can be found in my essay. All that Rachfahl says, he has taken from it and garbled (with some exceptions that are completely irrelevant). Anyone who disbelieves this, I recommend again to *read* my account impartially. You will see that after *this* critique I need not change *a single word*.

Weber's Notes

1   Rachfahl leaves this article conveniently aside, even though Troeltsch cites it.

2   In doing so, it probably did happen that on a few points (not all relevant to *his* theme) Troeltsch used formulations that do not quite correspond to my essays – as is scarcely avoidable when reproducing other people's views with such little space available. It fell to the dishonourable pettiness of a 'historical' critique to make the most of this circumstance: not once did Rachfahl feel himself in any *doubt* about the facts.

3   I stress at *Archiv* (XX:10/PE:44) that at least the direct connection between 'asceticism' and bourgeois wealth accumulation is often 'even *more* striking' in the ascetic sects (Quakers, Mennonites, and so on) than in Calvinism. And the reason why I discuss Calvinism first and at particular length (XXI:5–38/PE:98–128) I explain in detail at *Archiv* (XXI:36/PE:126) – namely, because in view of those impulses towards the *methodical* arrangement of life contained in its dogma, Calvinism seemed to me the most suitable and 'most consistent' antithesis to Catholicism and Lutheranism. But in any case, the 33 pages analysing Calvinism are followed by exactly as many on the other ascetic denominations (XXI:39–72/PE:128–44).

4   His only departure from me there is his use of inverted commas around 'ascetic'. (It is not that he is quoting.)

5   It is a moot point whether coining such words or symbols might not often be useful. I think it is to the credit of Georg Friedrich Knapp[xxvi] that he had the courage to do this extensively. Alfred Weber has also done it to remarkably clear effect in his book on the locations of industry.[xxvii] But in our readers it all too often meets with a disapproving shake of the head; and professorial vanity fundamentally resists any expression not coined by the particular *self* concerned.

6   Rachfahl's 'critique' can scarcely be esteemed of a high level when he challenges this in the following terms:

> As against the rich businessman, of whom Weber recounts that he could only with difficulty be persuaded to consume the oysters the doctor had prescribed for him, anyone can … think of more than one capitalist who undoubtedly possesses 'capitalist spirit' *in the usual sense* (nb!) … but who … happily allows himself to savour the fine shellfish. …

[xxvi]   Georg Friedrich Knapp (1842–1926): professor of economics at Strasbourg University until 1919 and a representative of the historical school. His main work was *Staatliche Theorie des Geldes* of 1905, in which he defined the value of money in postive–legal terms.

[xxvii]   Alfred Weber 1909

> I would love to think of delicatessen traders who close down for lack of custom due to ascetic habits suddenly invading the capitalist spirit.
>
> (Rachfahl 1909: 78)

I do not care what the 'usual sense' of the 'capitalist spirit' is, nor whether the 'Tiergarten quarter',[xxviii] the 'squirearchy' or the lieutenants and other young people with bulging wallets consume the most oysters. With this example (mentioned simply in passing!), I just wanted to illustrate a very specific inner relationship to acquisition and ownership: the feeling of 'responsibility' towards one's own property, which not only rejects 'irrational' expenditure but sees it as a curious kind of 'sin' (this has nothing to do with ordinary miserliness, which Rachfahl discusses elsewhere). It is an *ascetic* reservation about *consumption and enjoyment* as such.

7   As ever, it does not matter to Rachfahl if he says the exact opposite of things just to achieve a polemical effect. The same striving for profit for profit's sake which Rachfahl says at one place, in the case of Fugger, can very well have arisen from an 'ethical maxim for the conduct of life', he says at another place cannot be called 'ethical' at all, because he finds it reprehensible.

8   Consider all Rachfahl's comments on this.

9   Stupidly enough, for it is a matter of differences of *terminology* between Troeltsch and me, not of substance.

10   Even though in his statement of the contents of my essay, and occasionally later on, he cannot avoid mentioning other elements of my discussion.

11   The exceptional economic status of the [Catholic] Poles (whom I myself mentioned) is due to peculiarities of the Polish *nation*.

12   Shakespeare – an observer of Puritanism through the sharp eyes of hatred – evidently knew very well why he made his caricatured 'middle classes' ['*Mittelklassen*'] derive their caricatured agenda from the precept: 'It is written: work in your calling'.[xxix]

13   I had not looked at Petty since the time I was studying the history of trade, and I am grateful to my colleague H. Levy[xxx] for drawing my attention to this passage which I had forgotten.

14   I might just note here – a minor point – that obviously, when I contrasted a rigidly *intolerant* Calvinist New England with a *tolerant* Rhode Island, which was *apparently* less developed in terms of 'capitalist spirit' (see below), this was clearly intended to show that *despite* the intolerance of the former and the tolerance of the *latter*, this difference appears to have been to the advantage of the *in*tolerant area (which was provided with far fewer natural advantages). In my opinion, this was *because* the 'spirit' of Protestant asceticism was dominant in it to a greater degree. In any case, I said this only as a casual conjecture, which I could perhaps support with a few more points than I have made here, but without – as I again freely admit – being able to claim 'proof' of anything.

Allow me this opportunity to deal with some of Rachfahl's *factual* 'objections'. He seems completely unacquainted with the internal development of Pennsylvania, with the Quaker ethic and its tragic conflicts with the 'world', and likewise with the intensity of the mixture of asceticism and rationalism in the atmosphere there – which even in New York has lasted almost until the present (although Manhattan as a centre for immigration has for some

---

xxviii Wealthy central area of Berlin.

xxix *Henry VI*, Part 2, Act IV, Scene 2, Line 15. John Holland: 'True; and yet it is said, "Labour in thy vocation": which is as much as to say, "Let the magistrates be labouring men"; and therefore should we be magistrates'.

xxx Hermann Levy (1881–1949): professor of economics at Heidelberg from 1914.

time now lagged far behind Brooklyn in devoutness). *Every* good description by past European travellers attests to this intense atmosphere, and its traces still linger everywhere today in the part it plays in lifestyle and view of the calling. Rachfahl is equally unacquainted with the history of the New Englanders and their character, residues of which can still be felt today. I refer the reader to my (naturally *very* sketchy) essay in *Christliche Welt*. The agricultural 'capitalism' of the Episcopalian southern States was in *no* way different in the respects relevant to *my* problem from the 'capitalist' economy of the ancient world. From my own observations while with relatives in the southern States who live in old planters' houses,[xxxi] as well as from the well-known, sometimes excellent literature, I have gained a reasonably clear picture of the 'seigneurial' mixture of poverty-stricken slovenliness and aristocratic ostentation in business and life which governed this characteristically *unbourgeois* society. It stands in starkest contrast to the Puritan Yankee 'spirit'. New England is known to have come within a hair's breadth of falling into the hands of one of the numerous court favourites who sought to gain and exploit colonial land concessions – and even though no cotton plantations could have been established there, nobody knows what physiognomy North America might then have assumed without the settlements of the Pilgrim Fathers, which were joined further south by the Baptists, the Dutch and the Quakers. It certainly would have assumed nothing like that 'spirit' lent to it by these strata which has lasted in very significant traces until the present. That a 'capitalist', even a commercial, development in New England in the seventeenth century was not only an anachronism but geographically as good as impossible is not in doubt and I have never disputed this. I myself stated that it was remarkable for *precisely that reason* that there were *nevertheless* signs of commercial development beginning there after the Puritan immigration. As for Franklin, everybody knows that this small printer was far from being a capitalist on the 'grand scale' like Fugger. Furthermore, I myself emphasised this key fact that Franklin's capitalist 'spirit' developed here in an area still at the level of semi-barter economy (XX:33/PE:75). For these reasons, a critique even of Rachfahl's sort should have refrained from presenting me these things as 'objections'. As a historian, it is bad enough that he has no ability to distinguish the economic conditions of trade in a *colonial* country such as old New England from the European *Middle Ages* – as one of his sneering but in my opinion rather ridiculous remarks shows. And it is even worse that he should know nothing at all about the significance of the Huguenots in France and their industrial connections.

For a second time, I must 'concede' that Calvinism was unable to create a capitalist economy on the Hungarian Puszta [steppe land] in the seventeenth and eighteenth centuries; but equally I must stress that *even there* it shows its typical concomitants in the way Protestants chose their callings, as described at the outset of my essay.

Rachfahl is struck by the peculiar nature of Dutch capitalism and by the Dutch people's attitude to capitalism, which is indeed a very complex and interesting problem. Yet here too his eyes are fixed only on the big financiers who are *not* distinguished in any essentials from figures in all ages and countries and he develops only quite superficial sentiments. I therefore doubt that he knows more about this than I do – as in fact he kindly assures me – and I myself am anyway still far from clear about the matter. Certainly, everything he raises against me about merchant Arminianism I *myself* stated – as almost everywhere else – and I also mentioned precisely those same facts about Dutch art that he cites. But this issue is highly peripheral to my problem and it was never my wish to pursue it.

Let me mention something that goes deeper. The peculiarity of the Dutch 'spirit' at that time was certainly partly determined by the fact that the enclosure of new land by polders was one of the most profitable of all businesses. With a little exaggeration one can say that

---

[xxxi] See Marianne Weber 1988: 291–304.

the towns created the flat country out of themselves. Large quantities of capital were invested in farming (as well as in the colonial trade, which all Puritans were mildly suspicious of), and this was bound to affect the 'physiognomy' of the country. In important, though not all, respects, this prevented 'ascetic' Protestantism from making the impact for which it was well known elsewhere. For these farmers understandably differed from the traditional farming community on the rest of the continent, and also from the farmers of New England. They even had their significance for the art market: there are cases of sums being invested in paintings which represented a small fortune at that time and were certainly often of a speculative character. The consequences for Dutch art of this partial subduing of Puritanism in Holland is a very complex problem, and my casual remarks on the subject make no pretensions to anything. All the same, while the contrast between Rubens and Rembrandt and their respective conduct of life reflects no simple difference of milieu between them, it is far from being a coincidence. One recalls Baudelaire's lines about Rembrandt, which admittedly exaggerate to the point of caricature but still capture the basic outlook.[xxxii]

That a historian can speak of the Dordrecht Decrees almost as though they were an historical irrelevance can only indicate that he has no idea of modern Dutch ecclesiastical and political history.[xxxiii] The edifice of Dutch neo-Calvinism is certainly shot through with very modern insertions. But the Kuyper schism was decisive for the whole political constellation in Holland at the time, and was initiated by the genuinely 'Puritan' desire that the *congregation of communicants* be allowed to keep themselves 'pure' for the glory of God.[xxxiv] When one sees how the schism was based at all stages on concepts of justice and doctrines of faith which were developed before, during and after Dordrecht, one will find Rachfahl's assertion about this rather strange.[xxxv] One need only consider the printed records of Dutch church discipline at the time and the immense authority of the 'sacrosancta synodus'[xxxvi] whose followers for centuries could only utter its name on baring their heads. That Kuyper's neo-Calvinist church was first formed in 'unbelieving' Amsterdam could indeed be another 'coincidence', like Amsterdam's changing sides to join the Calvinist party

---

[xxxii] In 'Les Phares' from *Les fleurs du mal* Baudelaire describes Rembrandt in the following terms:
    Rembrandt, triste hôpital tout rempli de murmures,
    Et d'un grand crucifix décoré seulement,
    Où la prière en pleurs s'exhale des ordures,
    Et d'un rayon d'hiver traversé brusquement;
    This is in marked contrast to the stanza on Rubens:
    Rubens, fleuve d'oubli, jardin de la paresse,
    Oreiller de chair fraîche où l'on ne peut aimer,
    Mais où la vie afflue et s'agite sans cesse,
    Comme l'air dans le ciel et la mer dans la mer;
[xxxiii] The Dordrecht Decrees were the resolutions of the Synod of Dordrecht, 1618–19, which culminated in the formal victory of the orthodox Calvinists and the condemnation of the Arminian Remonstrants.
[xxxiv] Abraham Kuyper (1837–1920) was a conservative minister in the Dutch Reformed Church and leader of the Anti-Revolutionary Party in the Dutch Parliamentary Lower House. In 1892 he formed the *Gereformeerde Kerken*, also known as the Dutch Calvinist Church, which fought for a Christian politics against the modern movements of socialism and liberalism. He was also professor of theology at the Free University of Amsterdam, which he helped to found.
[xxxv] Weber is referring to Rachfahl's general downplaying of the Calvinist element in Dutch culture, his stress on the fact that Arminianism continued to exercise considerable influence after the Dordrecht Synod and on the legacy of Erasmian humanism.
[xxxvi] The Dordrecht Synod.

against Oldenbarnevelt,[xxxvii] as Rachfahl contends; but perhaps this remarkable modern 'coincidence' could prompt us to consider whether that event of 1618 might not have been grounded in something more than a *mere* temporary constellation of different 'cliques' in the Vroedshap.[xxxviii] (*Everywhere* in the world asceticism has almost *always* found itself in the *minority*: in Holland then and under Kuyper, in England under Cromwell, in Pennsylvania immediately after Penn, in France from the outset and similarly in Germany in the age of Pietism.) Judging by his remarks, Rachfahl scarcely seems to have heard of Puritan dissent in England and the role it played there right up until Cobden's anti-Corn Law agitation.[xxxix]

In the relationship between social *classes* and religious life that holds in almost all countries, it would be interesting to observe the gradual transformation of the divisions originally running *vertically* through the social stratification (and often including even Baptist groups) into *horizontal* ones. *This* is where the materialist 'interpretation' of history comes into play.

15   When Rachfahl asks how I *know* that the remark he quotes from Jacob Fugger (after me) expresses a *different* 'vocational ethic' (from the Puritan one), my answer is: because everyone who knows how a Puritan would express himself in the same situation also knows that in complete good faith he would have voiced his opinions *differently*. Without saying how, Rachfahl himself already *knows* that the Calvinist vocational ethic differs from Fugger's lifestyle in its view of profit and wealth as 'only of accessory importance'- just as I explained!

16   'Certainly Weber concedes that the Calvinist ethic turned out to be a force that willed the good but created evil – wealth in all its temptations.' To say of a writer he 'concedes' one of his own fundamental theses, quoted almost verbatim, is bound to mislead the reader, to say the least.

17   See my First Reply to Karl Fischer, 1907, *Archiv* (XXV:247, n.10) [see n.10, p.38, in this volume]. Rachfahl knows this piece too, as he occasionally cites it.

18   I have discussed Arminianism in the leading strata of the Dutch bourgeoisie with reference to Busken-Huët.[xl] It is a bit rich for Rachfahl to say I 'know' nothing of this when he himself offers little of any significance here.

19   Because of course it would not primarily be a matter of the distribution of *capital* and such like.

20   See my remarks at *Archiv* (XXVIII:263) and (XXIX:529).[xli]

[xxxvii]   Johan van Oldenbarnevelt (1547–1619) was the second founding father of the independent Dutch republic after William I the Silent, Prince of Orange, with whom he participated in the revolt against Spain in 1568 and the negotiation of the Union of Utrecht of 1579. In later years he became embroiled in a bitter quarrel with the strict Calvinist Counter-Remonstrants and was executed in 1619 on a charge of subverting religion.

[xxxviii]   The Amsterdam town council.

[xxxix]   Richard Cobden: see Part IV, trans. note xxxviii, p.122, in this volume.

[xl]   Conrad Busken-Huët (1826–86) was the most prominent Dutch literary critic of the nineteenth century, author of *Het Land van Rembrandt* ['Rembrandt's Country'], 1882–84.

[xli]   Weber is referring to his study of 1908–09, 'Zur Psychophysik der industriellen Arbeit', which makes extensive use of statistics. At the two places mentioned, Weber notes the prominence of Pietism among the female labour force of contemporary German industry. However, he adds that 'It must be sharply reiterated … that it is probably not confession as such which differentiates the modern factory labour force today, as seems to have been the case for the world of the bourgeoisie in the early capitalist period, but rather the intensity with which confessional affiliation, whether Catholic or Protestant, influences conduct of life in individual cases'.

21 'There *can be no doubt* that inner connections exist between Calvinism and capitalism' (but see above for Rachfahl's grave mistake of limiting these to just Calvinism) [see n.3, p.77, in this volume].

22 And of course even more so his assertion that what continued was the 'common Christian' Reformation morality (thereby including all the non- and anti-Calvinist movements).

23 From the emergence of the 'capitalist' spirit (in my sense!) in a place where the economic conditions were as unfavourable as possible (*still!*), I concluded that the kind of methodical conduct of life which then prevailed in New England and Pennsylvania contained in *itself* the impetus for capitalist development. That such a seed then needed the appropriate 'conditions' in order to play a part (and note: just a *part!*) in the genesis of a capitalist 'economic system' was obvious; even so, I stated this *too* for safety's sake (XX:53f/PE:91f; XXI:110/PE:183). I thought it would be superfluous to add this, but now I see I am mistaken!

24 I do not understand where I am supposed to have spoken of an '*absolute*' dominance of Puritanism in English economic life. The bourgeois–capitalist middle classes fought on two fronts: on the one hand, initially against the 'squirearchy' and 'merry old England' – this was a quite explicit struggle of 'asceticism', in which the Crown intervened through the Book of Sports;[xlii] and on the other, against the seventeenth-century court monopolists and big financiers – one thinks of the well-known moves of the Long Parliament in this direction.[xliii] As I would have needed to show in the continuation of my article, this latter struggle was supported by a very specific theory of the '*justum pretium*', consistent with Puritan ethics.[xliv]

25 But – God knows – I did not *assert* it to be a work all on its own in every or even in most vehicles of 'capitalist spirit' (in my sense), as he claims.

26 He even realises that what I tried to explain was the *disappearance* of the combination of motives at work in ascetic Protestantism's heyday (what he attacks is my mode of explanation). But just for this reason, his 'even today' once again exemplifies his fondness for vaguely impressive-sounding turns of phrase that serve nothing. The fact that *he himself* contrasts the lifestyle of present-day large-scale capitalism with Calvinist capitalism – in just the sense he found in my work, expressed in different words – completes this picture of hollow rhetoric.

[xlii] In 1617 James I issued a *Book of Sports* licensing games and dancing on Sundays. The Book ordered that 'provided it be without impediment or neglect of divine service', the people should not be 'discouraged from any lawful recreation, such as dancing, either men or women; archery for men, leaping, vaulting or any other such harmless recreation, nor from having of May-games, Whitsun-ales and Morris dances ...' (quoted in Sharpe 1992:352). Despite mounting opposition from Puritan magistrates, clergymen and JPs since Elizabethan times who had sought to suppress such activities, the order was reissued by Charles I in 1633, amid great controversy.

[xliii] The last sittings of the English Parliament before the outbreak of Civil War and the execution of Charles I, November 1640 to April 1653.

[xliv] In *Economy and Society* (1978b: vol. II, 873) Weber notes how the old medieval theory of the '*justum pretium*' or 'just price' of labour for farm workers gradually ceased to be understood in terms of what was appropriate for the subsistence of the worker and was instead redefined in terms of what market competition would bear. This redefinition of the 'natural' price of labour reached its height with the Puritans' assault on private monopolists in the seventeenth century. Weber writes: 'The price which was to be rejected as "unnatural" was now one which did not rest on the competition of the free market, i.e. the price which was influenced by monopolies or other arbitrary human intervention. Throughout the whole puritanically influenced Anglo-Saxon world this principle has had a great influence up to the very present'.

27   My emphases.

28   Sombart (*Archiv*, XXIX:701) rightly notes the big entrepreneur, Rathenau,[xlv] when he quotes him (from the latter's *Reflexionen*, [1908]) as saying that he, Rathenau, has never yet known 'a truly great businessman and entrepreneur for whom earning money was the main point of his calling, and I would go so far as to claim that whoever thinks only of personal profit can never be a great businessman'.[xlvi] (Franklin would have said just the same, quite regardless of his 'sermon', and so too would the Puritans – they above all. For all these men, gaining wealth is 'something accessory', to use Rachfahl's word.)

29   I have given far more graphic examples of this than just 'pious endowments.' Actions of this kind were quite usual in almost equal degrees among Calvinists and Protestants in general, though from very different motives, indeed characteristically different motives.

30   As I have stressed very emphatically, in any eventual completion of my essay, the reverse causal relationship will have to be dealt with, whereby religious life is determined by economic conditions. I stressed that in doing so I would probably be accused of 'capitulating to historical materialism', just as much as I have been accused of 'exaggerating the influence of religious elements'. Rachfahl even uses the word 'monstrous' for this aspect of my 'thesis' – though this hardly accords with his *appropriating* its content *himself*. Let me remark, in passing, that the religious influence is of a quite different and more fundamental significance even in the *political* field than the impression given by those 'nothing-but-politicians' historians who understand by the 'great powers' only the great battalions that the good Lord accompanies on the *battlefield*. No such 'power' has ever managed to disable this one dictum of the Bible, 'We must obey God rather than men',[xlvii] *as long as* it governed the faith of resolute men, however much in a minority, as the Puritans almost universally were. Those who fought on behalf of *Kultur* in the seventeenth and the nineteenth centuries foundered on this dictum's power, and on both occasions the consequences of their defeat lasted for generations.[xlviii] Of course, this is very far from having been the only foundation of political individualism (here I take this expression to be unambiguous). But the fact that our present political individualism lacks this element and *must* lack it, accounts for far more than those clever people will ever even dream of. In Germany, thanks among other things to Lutheranism, it in part always *has* been lacking and in part has had only *passive* consequences.

31   I find it simply unbelievable that Rachfahl should suppose I overlooked the role of 'agonistic drives' in the concept of the 'spirit' of capitalism, when I went out of my way to show how today these 'drives' have in many ways *taken the place* of the moribund ascetic 'spirit'. It is not illegitimate to speak here of 'drives'. For an illustration, consider my

---

xlv   Walter Rathenau (1867–1922): industrialist, president of the company AEG, and foreign minister responsible for German war reparations after 1919. In his numerous writings, Rathenau emphasised humankind's need for spiritual sustenance beyond materialism and mechanisation and for a new kind of communitarian economy beyond both capitalism and socialism.

xlvi   Sombart 1909; see also Sombart 1913:217/172.

xlvii   Acts of the Apostles, chap. 5, line 29.

xlviii   A reference to the struggle of the Prussian state under Bismarck against the Roman Catholic church in the 1870s, the so-called *Kulturkampf*, which ended with the repeal of Bismarck's May Laws in 1887 and the defeat of his attempt to curtail the influence of the Catholic Conservatives on education in Prussia, a conflict echoing similar struggles between church and state in seventeenth-century Europe. See Part IV, trans. note xli, p.123, in this volume.

example at *Archiv* (XXI:109, n.85a/PE:283, n.115), as well as Rockefeller's testimony before the Industrial Commission (on this see Sombart, *Archiv*, XXIX, 710).[xlix]

32   It is purely a terminological difference between Sombart and me when he explains the typical 'tendencies' of entrepreneurs that arise out of the force of circumstances and that lead them to purposive action in terms of the 'psychology' of entrepreneurialism (*Archiv*, XXIX:709),[l] whereas I term all such causal elements 'pragmatic' or 'rational' (inasmuch as they derive from means unavoidably necessary for desired economic ends). Sombart's account brings out the decisive points of the matter very well. However, I still have some reservations about the appropriateness of the term 'psychology' for this analysis of action, which I set out at *Archiv* (XXVII:546ff.).[li] For instance, when talking about 'stock market psychology' one tends to think of 'irrational' phenomena, phenomena which can*not* be derived rationally from the trading situation.

A wealth of explanations and examples could of course be added to Sombart's discussion. A particular case in point is the 'pragmatic' limits surrounding what he has called 'calculativeness' (*'Rechenhaftigkeit'*). I once happened to become acquainted with the internal affairs of one of the very biggest commercial concerns that had grown out of a family business and now engaged in nearly every imaginable form of wholesale trading in three large trading centres in Europe and two overseas. Its individual 'branches' varied unbelievably *greatly* in quantity and intensity of work, as did their capital requirements and their contributions to the total profit (which all went into the one coffer, just as in medieval times). Moreover, one member of the family, a most astute businessman, had tired of his office and preferred to live in Paris, from where he travelled whenever important meetings came up. Despite this, the profit, which ran into very high figures, was shared out equally per head with only one distinction: between a double or single share. Double shares went to the head of the largest branch, who worked in a truly gargantuan office, and to another branch head who had to reside in a particularly uncongenial place overseas. All other partners received single shares, including the 'occasional' worker in Paris. A more exact calculation was certainly seen as possible, but simply because of the profit's *size*, as too 'inconvenient', 'petty' and 'unnecessary'. Admittedly, in the case of a highly valued relative and intimate friend of the company head who was indispensable to the business but whose smaller share in the business had been forfeited during a crisis and who now 'served' as an 'employee' (attorney), it was considered that fixing his salary higher than usual, higher than he could achieve *elsewhere*, would be against all 'business principles' and impossible because other employees could then demand the same. He should not have

---

[xlix]   Sombart (1909) cites Rockefeller as the epitome of the tendency to 'limitless acquisition'. He quotes Rockefeller's testimony before the Industrial Commission of 1900, which decided on the future of his Standard Oil Company: 'As the business grew and markets were obtained at home and abroad more persons and capital were added to the business and new corporate agencies were obtained or organised, the object being always the same, to extend our business by furnishing the best and cheapest products'. Sombart comments: 'I have reproduced this testimony of Rockefeller before the Industrial Commission at length because it seems to me to embody in its most classical form the bare tendency to limitless acquisition. The monomaniacal element is here splendidly depicted. Capital is meaninglessly heaped upon capital: why? because(!) business grows. "Extension of the business" – this is the governing outlook. Cheapness and quality of production are means to this end!'. Weber's example at *Archiv* (XXI:109, n.85a/PE:283, n.115) is his reference to the 'leading dry-goods man of an Ohio city' whose German son-in-law cannot understand the man's obsession with expanding his shop.
[l]   Sombart 1909.
[li]   Weber 1908b.

'expected anything else': *his* salary was part of the *costs* and was therefore governed by purely economic, 'calculative' considerations. Nonetheless, once the 'profit' had exceeded a certain threshold, such 'calculativeness' came to an end, because from the 'pragmatic' [purposive–rational] point of view, it was seen as no longer indispensable to the existence of the business. *Such* cases, of which there are many, we can explain rationally, without recourse to any 'psychology', in terms of the 'nature' of 'capitalism' through the categories of 'means' and 'end'. However, from the *historical* standpoint this rational deduction is not alone *sufficient* because elements explicable in terms of the economic *system* become wedded to other elements of most heterogeneous provenance that help shape the 'spirit' informing this system at any one time. Still, it remains true that categories such as 'acquisitive drive', 'passion for profit' and the like are *not at all* satisfactory for analysing the 'capitalist spirit', *whichever way* one understands this concept – as Sombart has also emphasised very correctly.

33   On the concept of 'ideal type', see my essay at *Archiv* (XIX).[lii]

34   Since then I have changed my terminology. Earlier I was not inclined to use the term 'capitalist' to describe more than occasional phenomena in the economy of the ancient world and therefore had doubts about speaking of ancient 'capitalism'. Now I think differently, as can be seen in my 'Agrarverhältnisse im Altertum', 1909.[liii]

35   I myself emphasised at *Archiv* (XXVI:279, n.3)[liv] that because of my not having completed the project 'hasty readers will easily see this essay as something self-contained'. However, a 'critic' has no right to be one of those hasty readers. Merely my short sketch in *Christliche Welt* will show anyone that my *Archiv* essay approached the problem first deliberately from the *most difficult* aspect concerning inner habitus and did not discuss the powerful influence of upbringing and discipline in the sects up until the present but only hinted at it. When Rachfahl emphasises the significance of *upbringing*, one need not know much about the effect of *Pietistic* principles of education to realise that here too quite specific influences of 'ascetic' Protestantism were at work that were in keeping with the developments I portrayed.

36   Note that modern capitalism is indeed all I have been talking about. It would of course have been wise to make this explicit in the title and in my nomenclature throughout; but I did not do this for the reason above (n.35 [see previous note]).

37   The way Rachfahl censures my brief remarks on the growth of bourgeois 'comfort' in contrast to the seigneurial lifestyle I find truly small-minded – one can scarcely call it anything else. This contrast is known to every beginner in cultural history. 'Boundaries' between contrasting phenomena are fluid *everywhere* in history. Some historians seem unable to grasp that it is necessary to make sharp conceptual distinctions precisely *because* of this. I refer the reader to my discussion in the *Handwörterbuch der Staatswissenschaften*, 1909.

[lii]   Weber 1904.
[liii]   Weber 1909.
[liv]   See Part II, Weber's note 3, p.49, in this volume.

Part IV

CHAPTER 7

Felix Rachfahl's Reply to Weber, 1910

From the *Internationale Wochenschrift für Wissenschaft, Kunst und Technik*, 1910 4th quarter, pp. 689–794

Summary

Like Weber's first Reply to Rachfahl, Rachfahl's second essay contains extended denials and disclaimers of the positions imputed to him. Rachfahl insists that Weber and Troeltsch *have* borrowed from each other, consciously or not, and that far from 'dishonourably' playing them off against each other, he was merely seeking to determine differences between them. He denies asserting that the Protestant vocational ethic played no role whatsoever or that Enlightenment political culture and tolerance in the seventeenth and eighteenth centuries were exclusive causes of capitalist growth. He points out that he never ascribed to Weber the 'foolish–doctrinaire thesis' of 'deriving' the capitalist spirit 'or even capitalism' itself from the Reformation, indeed had quoted these very words of Weber in his review. He had merely counselled against exaggerating the influence of religious factors, arguing that we must try to establish the precise *degree* to which capitalism could have developed under Protestant influences. In focusing on Calvinism, he can hardly be accused of fixing on something peripheral to Weber's interests; and in arguing for more exactness and clarity in the causal linkage of the two elements, he cannot be caricatured as asking for some means of measurement or quantification.

A central plank of Rachfahl's argument is that Weber's numerous hedgings and qualifications of his thesis so narrows down its scope as to make its relevance to modern capitalism too tenuous to be of any great explanatory value. Weber offers a 'case of the co-existence of Calvinism and capitalism without any causal connection'. Inasmuch as it only examines the 'practical significance of Puritanism' (in Troeltsch's paraphrase), it essentially renounces its claim to explain capitalist development in other key Protestant countries such as Switzerland and the Netherlands and among the French Huguenots; and in limiting himself to the smaller middling classes of England and America in the seventeenth century, Weber covers only a small fraction of the 'modern capitalism' implied in his reference to the 'specifically modern capitalist spirit'. If we describe the way a cobbler manages his finances as illustrative of 'capitalist spirit', the following question arises:

> Should not investigations into the history of the 'capitalist spirit' take rather as their object those circumstances where capitalism has really been the substrate of this 'capitalist spirit'? However much the 'bourgeois middle classes' may have sought to improve their social and economic position, they did not as such become the bearers of capital and of the capitalist system. It would therefore seem appropriate for questions concerned in the widest sense with the history of capital to concentrate primarily on the 'great financiers' and 'economic supermen', i.e. on the accumulation of great stocks of capital and the 'spirit' that guided this [...] Even if there can be capitalist spirit without a capitalist system, it is only worthwhile for the economic history of modern times to trace those manifestations of the capitalist spirit that contributed toward, and were carried along by the tendency toward, accumulation of capital and the creation, maintenance and development of a capitalist economic system.
>
> (1910:247, 255)

Rachfahl points out that while few will deny the influence of Puritanism in America, whether it became the soil for the emergence of a capitalist economy there in the eighteenth century is another matter. Hard work, parsimony, thrift and occupational commitment does not necessarily constitute 'capitalist spirit': one might as well say the same thing of German craftsmen in the Middle Ages. Thus Rachfahl believes Weber's ascetic capitalists are insufficiently *typical* of modern capitalist lifestyles to merit the significance he awards them.

On the question of 'inner-worldly asceticism', Rachfahl still regards Weber's use of this term as a misnomer. The idea that after the Reformation 'every man was expected to lead his life like a monk' remains only a figure of speech and cannot form the basis of a scientific hypothesis. Rachfahl notes that according to prominent Reformation historians such as Gustav Kawerau and F. Kattenbusch, the decisive feature of Protestantism in contrast to Catholicism was precisely the absence of asceticism. Calvinism in particular was not ascetic in any marked sense: Calvin did not preach against life's pleasures as such – they were, after all, God's gifts – but against excess.

Concerning religion and capitalism in Holland, Rachfahl stresses that despite the victory of orthodox Calvinism at the Synod of Dordrecht in 1618–19, the more secular influence of Arminianism persisted for a long time afterwards in Dutch society. He cites the remark of the notable Dutch historian, Busken-Hüet, that Holland's religion is essentially 'the religion of Erasmus'. Calvinism was certainly not the only governing element in the rebellion against Spain. According to Groen van Prinsterer, the distribution of Calvinists and Lutherans among the wealthy at Antwerp was roughly equal and the same across different professions. Parrying Weber's appeal to William Petty's observations on Holland, Rachfahl points out that Petty only says the Dutch regarded it as their duty to God to show 'labour and industry': this is not the same as any 'ascetic vocational ethic'. Luther, too, said it was man's duty to work and not be idle. This again constitutes no 'capitalist spirit' or 'habitus', and holds just as much of the ordinary day labourer working from hand to mouth as of the Puritan bookkeeper. Rachfahl also notes significantly that Weber illicitly interpolates the phrase 'Puritan dissenters' into his second quotation from Petty about the Dutch's rejection of 'voluptuaries and men of extreme wealth and power', when in fact Petty is specifically referring to the Dutch rebels at the time of the revolt against Spain.

Rachfahl's final argument is that Weber equivocates between his vocational ethic as the '*constitutive* factor' in the capitalist spirit and as 'one factor among others'. These two phrases cannot be combined without ambiguity. Instead, Rachfahl proposes that thrift, parsimony and ethical commitment to one's vocation should be seen as constant elements throughout history, and as only intensified during the Reformation period, not as products of the Reformation. The Reformation merely removed ascetic–monastic hindrances to the flourishing of the vocational ethics that already existed. Moreover, there have always been capitalists either more or less 'impulsive' or more or less 'rationalised'. A certain degree of rationalisation is always necessary to regulate and organise the capitalist's acquisitive drive, but this rationalisation need not affect the capitalist's entire conduct of life; it need only affect his manner of acquiring objects so that it starts to take on a speculative–calculative character. Asceticism cannot be seen as the root of this 'calculativeness'. Weber also exaggerates the Catholic Renaissance capitalist's need for 'appeasement' so as to 'feel at one with his actions'; and his notion that ascetic Protestantism created the corresponding 'soul' and 'habitus' of modern capitalism remains insufficiently scientific.

CHAPTER 8

Weber's Second Reply to Rachfahl, 1910

From the *Archiv für Sozialwissenschaft und Sozialpolitik*, vol. 31, pp. 554–99

Professor Rachfahl has replied to me once again in four issues of the *Internationale Wochenschrift*. Instead of honestly admitting his gross errors and superficial reading, he partly takes a new turn and partly compounds these errors even more desperately, and generally continues in just the way I was compelled to characterise previously.[1] At the end we find him assuring us in a way that strikingly recalls the habits of American party hacks during an election campaign that he has 'fulfilled' his 'purpose' and 'burst the bubble of soap on the Neckar'. At another point he even avers that he, Rachfahl, will seem to *me* 'like the vulture that feeds upon the carcass of his opponent'. Well now, we shall see that this 'carcass' is in fact still quite alive and kicking; and in its eyes Rachfahl looks very unlike an eagle or anything of that nature, but rather, as always, in both his reply and review, like a very light-feathered and yet all too heavily pedantic species of writer, against whom it is not even possible to bear any ill-will – for all one's head-shaking – because his often quite unbelievable lack of any sense of the need for literary honesty stems from the quandary he has fallen into, outdone only by the equally incredible naivety of his quite unwavering conviction of being always in the right. Now that I have followed the wishes of my friends and taken on this sterile and irksome business of tackling his purely *semantic* sophistry, which disguises the clear facts of the case, I shall have to carry it through. In what follows, then, I shall of necessity (1) establish the 'spirit' of Rachfahl's polemic once more – and in order to follow him into all the nooks and crannies of his case, this will, unfortunately and in the circumstances unavoidably, be a rather prolonged discussion which I leave to every reader with no particular interest in it to skip – and then (2) for my part – in the face of the confusion caused by Rachfahl and now increased by his avoidance of any admission of injustice – draw together again in a few pages some threads of my *real* 'thesis' which Rachfahl has stubbornly ignored, simply for the benefit of those who have not carefully examined my essays. For others, this will be superfluous, but of course these are a vanishing minority.

I

Since I called Rachfahl's polemic 'professorial', he thinks I try to disparage his quality as a 'professor', and thereby presumably claim some 'better' position for myself. This is an error that typifies his lack of comprehension in the matter at hand. However, in the context of this otherwise quite sterile discussion of ours, it is, nevertheless, an instructive error. For while I believe he is both a 'professor' *and* the author of an unusually 'professorial' essay, everyone knows that not everything a professor writes (and, God be thanked, this also includes Rachfahl) possesses that familiar admixture of hair-splitting pedanticism and petty superiority that describes the essence of the 'professorial' – any more than everything a newspaper editor writes possesses that equally familiar quality of the 'journalistic' (in inverted commas!). Similarly, everyone knows that any state that functions according to bureaucratic forms is not just for that reason governed by the 'spirit of bureaucracy'. If this were so, every army (and the state it serves) organised after the model of the German or French armies would have to be informed by the 'militaristic spirit' (the contrasting case one thinks of here is Italy). No German *Gewerkverein* possessing the same organisation as a French 'syndicat' or an English 'trade union' has to be characterised by the spirit of 'syndicalisme' or the spirit of 'trades unionism' (the choice of these two being left open here), any more than a country with a colonial empire need invariably be governed by the 'spirit of imperialism', or finally a capitalistically organised economy by the 'spirit of capitalism'. (And such an economy certainly need not be governed by that specific spirit I claimed distinguishes modern capitalism from that of antiquity and the Middle Ages, above all in its heroic early period.) However, the reason why we nevertheless speak of such a 'spirit' in the context of these systems lies – to repeat – in the fact that the attitude designated in this way, or several possible attitudes, seem to us somehow to be specifically 'adequate' to just those forms of organisation. For *inner* reasons, they seem to possess an 'elective affinity' to them, but without necessarily being thereby bound to them in every single case or even in the majority of cases or on average. It is, for example, a typical occurrence everywhere in history that a state or other social institution continues to exist in just the same forms but appears to be changed in its 'meaning' for historical life, in its 'significance' for cultural history. In such cases, whenever we speak of a change in its 'spirit', as we habitually do, we naturally have an unconditional duty to clarify on each occasion what we understand by this and what concrete causes determined the change. In my case, my task was to reveal what I believed was *one* particularly important series of causes that conditioned the formation of again *one* particularly important constitutive *component* of the 'spirit' of the modern capitalist economy. So my object was one colouring of this spirit, specifically different in important ways from ancient and medieval times. This was the task I expressly set myself.

Since Rachfahl now behaves as though I only constructed this careful delimitation of my task *ex post* (and of course as he would like: because of his 'critique'), confident that 99 in a 100 of his audience has not read either my essay or Reply, nor will read them, I would just like to remind readers once more of the following. At *Archiv* (XXI:107/PE:180) I described the result of my studies (I even quoted these passages in my Reply!) as being that '*one* (nb!) of the fundamental elements' of the 'capitalist spirit' had the origin I asserted: the origin of the specifically 'bourgeois ethic of the calling' (XXI:105/PE:176) with the particular 'ascetic' characteristic that accompanies it and that has retained its significance against the powerful spiritual resistance of tradition – until our present-day capitalism, resting as it does on purely mechanical foundations, was able to *shed* this support (XXI:108/PE:181f.). At *Archiv* (XX:54/PE:91) I described the hypothesis of 'deriving' both the capitalist economic *system and* the capitalist '*spirit*' (in *my* sense of the word) *solely* from the Reformation as 'foolish'; and at *Archiv* (XXI:4, n.1–2/PE:97) I also stated explicitly the truism that religious–psychological factors were only able to foster capitalist development directly in the context of numerous other, especially natural-geographic, 'conditions'. Finally, in my Reply to a review similar in character to Rachfahl's,[i] I again made clear as early as 1908 – in order to preclude *every* 'absolutisation' of the causal constellation I discussed – that my studies analyse *exclusively* the development of an ethical 'lifestyle' adequate to the emergent capitalism of modern times. If, therefore, others have 'overestimated the scope of my discussion', this is not my fault. I added that after finishing my essays I could quite possibly be accused of 'capitulating to historical materialism'.[ii] Rachfahl even *cited* the short polemical essay in which I made these last remarks. Yet in response to my complaint that though he knew all this he felt no obligation to take it into account, he now has the astonishing impertinence to assure the readership of the *Internationale Wochenschrift* that he *knew nothing* of my comments on this score, indeed that even today he 'has been unable to find them'. I leave it to the reader what expression I would need to use for this 'inability', were I to react in any other way than to shrug my shoulders at a person so seized by the mania of needing to be right at any price, even the price of literary honesty. I simply note further that wherever it suits

---

[i] See Part II, Fischer, pp.43–51, in this volume.
[ii] See Part II, Webers's n.5, p.50, in this volume.

his purposes, he prattles on *even now* about 'Weber's view of the Calvinist (sic) monopoly (sic) over the (sic) development of capitalism' – and after all his protestations that he was representing my views 'correctly'! On the next page he assures us that he 'did not at all imply' that I 'derived the capitalist economic system from religious causes'. It makes no difference here that he put an 'excerpt' from my essay at the beginning of his review with an account of its contents which in most respects was accurate, though by no means all. For even where it was accurate, he forgot what he said even in the next column, as I pointed out to him again and again and shall continue to do. Quite simply, he was, and is, in a dilemma. His article took shape in the way we see because he wanted to write an article on Calvin in which to show off his critical superiority as a historical 'specialist' to an 'outsider',[iii] though in an area where he first had to obtain 'material' for himself. Then he finds that for reasons of disciplinary patriotism he has to be 'in the right' in any way possible and has to force my 'thesis' to fit his 'critique'. It is not good to go about literary business in this 'spirit'.

As a mark of the integrity of his polemic, I note how graciously Rachfahl tells my 'friends and disciples' (whom he obviously thinks are to be pitied) that I 'roughly disown' them – presumably in order to rescue myself from his polemic?[2] Perhaps he thinks these funny tricks [*Mätzchen*] of his – really quite silly in a serious piece of work, though his review and reply both teem with them – constitute some kind of 'instructive nastiness'? But now to the matter at hand.

Rachfahl's reply begins with a lengthy sally against Troeltsch's reply to his critique.[iv] Whether Troeltsch will find it worth taking the trouble to answer it, I do not know. For myself, seeing that I am now answering, I have an interest in drawing attention to the following. In his original review, after giving some examples, actual or alleged, of religious conditions having *no* effect on political events, Rachfahl wrote: 'From all this, one thing is evident: how little political, economic and secular developments in general (sic) are bound by religious doctrines when such doctrines reach beyond the domain of the purely religious'.[3] *Now* he writes: 'I (Rachfahl) have highlighted particular concrete cases in which the influence of religious moments ... has been exaggerated; from these, however, I have drawn no general conclusion of the kind imputed to me by Troeltsch (sic),[4] and the way he foists such a conclusion on me (sic) I prefer not to characterise here as I would have to choose very bitter words (sic)'. Such is the character of Rachfahl's reply, as we shall see again. Might I not 'use bitter words' myself? I am amused, but sincerely regret having taken seriously a confused critic[5] who feels such anxiety

---

iii English in original.
iv Troeltsch 1910.

when confronted with *his own* assertions. Any other polemical purpose than that of *appearing* to be right 'in public' is clearly incomprehensible to Rachfahl.

To continue, in my First Reply to Rachfahl (*Archiv*, XXX:177) I reject his incorrect statements about the relations between Sombart's works and mine and refer to *my* express and exhaustive remarks on this point in the essay itself at *Archiv* (XX:19, n.1/PE:198, n.14).ᵛ Rachfahl's answer to this is: 'That Sombart's book on capitalism influenced Weber's thesis is reported by Troeltsch (sic). How (sic) should I have supposed that he (Troeltsch) … was misinformed?'

Further, as far as links between Troeltsch's works and mine are concerned, both he and I have *explained* that (i) neither of us is responsible for the other's work and why, and that (ii) my 'thesis' is no argument for his 'theses' and vice versa – each of us could be completely right in the positions taken while the other completely wrong. However, we have also explained that (iii) my results certainly represent a *supplement* to his results and tally well with them, which (iv) he has accordingly acknowledged by *reviewing* them, in the course of which (v) he made a few minor errors on *isolated* points quite unimportant for *his* purposes (which Rachfahl then attempted to capitalise on in an exceedingly small-minded way, as I stressed).⁶ I described it as 'dishonourable' that someone calling himself a 'critic' should pretend that what to everyone are obviously *terminological* differences between Troeltsch and me were actually *substantive* ones (and exploiting Troeltsch's in themselves quite immaterial errors in rendering some of my formulations). Yet on the next page he speaks of 'Troeltsch–Weber concepts' *precisely at those points* where he has exploited our differences (concerning 'asceticism').⁷ Even now Rachfahl occasionally behaves in the same way. But when he now even says that Troeltsch and I 'recognise (sic) that they associate different ideas with the word "asceticism"', his attempt to claim the credit for this 'recognition' will deceive only someone who has not read my or Troeltsch's works. Troeltsch was speaking quite explicitly about Lutheran asceticism while I quite explicitly described my quite different concept of asceticism as not only *not* applicable to Lutheranism (and various other Protestant communities) but as standing in sharpest contrast to it. No spirit needed 'rise from the grave' – or rather inkwell – to confirm *this* difference. Even the hastiest reader imaginable was bound to see (and Rachfahl *did* see) that this was a matter of differences of terminology, not of argument. So, without wasting another word, I will leave it to anyone with the time to compare these clear facts of the matter with the little tricks by which Rachfahl would *still* like to 'know better', even after both Troeltsch and I have explained our positions explicitly.⁸

ᵛ   See Part III, trans. note iv, p.62, in this volume.

And in order finally to end this rather silly controversy over terminology, let me remind readers that I *did* explain, and will willingly explain *again*, that the expression 'inner-worldly asceticism' can be exchanged for *any* other one might choose. As usual, Rachfahl says nothing of this to his readers, and in what can only be described as his usual 'spiteful' tone speaks of my 'fatherly joy' in coining expressions. Naturally, one cannot substitute alternative expressions where actual differences of *fact* are concerned. I shall deal with these later in my positive résumé (section II). For the time being, I must carry on showing in a purely negative fashion how throughout Rachfahl's reply the same kind of sloppy polemic tries to wriggle out of any honest confession of weaknesses.

Rachfahl protests that he did not represent *tolerance* as a carrier of the capitalist spirit, nor as a cause of capitalist development; and yet he now assures us again, even on *the same page* (and quite apart from the remarks in his review which I reproduced *absolutely* correctly), that 'It (tolerance) was the soil that the capitalist spirit *required* in order to put down firm roots and not wither away; this is not a construct but historical fact'.[9] No, if one wants to substitute 'condition' here for 'cause', to comply with Rachfahl's quibbling, this is *neither* fact *nor* construct (not even meaningful construct!) but totally superficial assertion, proving that the real problems have not been thought through. Capitalist spirit in *Rachfahl's* sense of the word ran riot in Venice, Genoa, Florence, Flanders and large parts of France towards the end of the Middle Ages, and even in Seville in the sixteenth and seventeenth centuries, without being harmed in the slightest by the then taken-for-granted intolerance. Where, for example, the sources of Seville's atrophy really lay (insofar as Catholicism was uniquely involved in this, which it certainly was) can be seen clearly enough in this strictly Catholic town's conflicts with church and state – familiar to everyone with any knowledge of Spanish economic history. Here, too, intolerance did *nothing* to harm the 'economic supermen', whom Rachfahl identifies as the real 'carriers' of the capitalist spirit, the big bankers and monopolists, known since the beginning of history to have fairly easily come to terms with intolerance. Despite intolerance, the Fuggers and the big capitalists of Seville and elsewhere made just as splendid business deals in the sixteenth century as the Peruzzi and Bardi and their like in the intolerant Middle Ages and similarly the big English and Dutch capitalists in both tolerant and intolerant countries. Conversely, the practically extremely wide-ranging and long-lasting 'tolerance' of the Norman state was little able to draw away the centre of gravity of medieval Mediterranean capitalism from the devout and 'intolerant' cities of northern Italy into the Sicilian cities – as little as the in practice completely tolerant (within the limits of 'reason of state') Roman Empire arrested the decline of the ancient capitalist 'spirit' and ancient capitalism. And finally there is the circumstance (which Rachfahl's zeal makes him once again forget) that

Protestant England, both Anglican and Presbyterian (and likewise New England), was in principle just as intolerant as a Catholic state[10] but put nothing in the way of a growing capitalist spirit there (in Rachfahl's general ahistorical sense). For wherever they were not actually stamped out, the Puritans' mere *existence*, whether officially tolerated or not, contributed just as much to the development of that 'nuance' (to use Rachfahl's word) of the capitalist spirit that I so emphasise as did their *dominance*, whether this was itself tolerant or intolerant in outlook. By contrast, what the intolerant Catholic states snuffed out was precisely *this* 'nuance' [of the capitalist spirit], *not* the actual existence of those Rachfahlian high financiers. One thinks of France after the repeal of the Edict of Nantes, as contemporaries, and famously Colbert, best knew.[vi] In a word, Protestantism, especially ascetic Protestantism, whether tolerated, tolerant or intolerant, *helped* the capitalist spirit take root *both* in its general (Rachfahlian) sense *and* in my specific sense. By contrast, Catholicism, tolerated or dominant, has *never fostered* it – or where and how, may I ask?

According to Rachfahl's current admission, tolerance helped the capitalist spirit 'take root' only where it benefited it *directly*. However, this *can* only have been the case where there were certain population groups whose *religious beliefs led them to become affected by intolerance* and *thereby became carriers of that specific spirit*; and by Rachfahl's own comments, this was certainly *not* the case with those great financial people who have existed just as much in tolerant as intolerant periods and states. To complete this reasoning: intolerant Catholicism was fatal for the capitalist 'spirit' in modern times *only* on two counts. It was fatal, first, where it stamped out the *heretical carriers of the bourgeois business spirit*. Here let me repeat that it was *not* fortuitous (as contemporaries such as Petty knew) that those carriers were, κατ᾽ ἐξοχήν,[vii] the ascetic heretics, or those suspected of heresy – even in the Middle Ages (for example the Humiliati[viii] and similar groups) but especially in the Reformation and Counter-Reformation. And, second, it was fatal where, through forced monastic foundations, it eliminated wealth accumulation from private business (this wealth accumulation having been fostered in the monasteries *too* by ascetic *methodical* life practices, as I pointed out) and, from the viewpoint of *private* capital, drove it into a 'dead canal' [*toten Kanal*], thereby sucking *out* of the world and transferring to monastic cells precisely those *people* who by

---

vi   Edict of Nantes: law promulgated in 1598 by Henry IV, granting religious and civil liberties to Huguenot Protestants, but repealed in 1685 by Louis XIV. Charles Colbert, marquis de Croissy (1625–96), was Louis XIV's secretary of state for foreign affairs.

vii   Pre-eminently, *par excellence*.

viii   The Humiliati: an unorthodox Catholic group, active in Lombardy from the twelfth to sixteenth centuries, dedicated to living a life of extreme poverty and self-sacrifice.

their at once inborn and acquired rational–ascetic character would have been specifically *predisposed* to make a 'calling' of their 'divinely ordained' work. So, the significance of tolerance for capitalist development, taken *independently* of the question of which type of religiosity it benefited, was exactly as I described it in my essay, which Rachfahl attempted to reproduce but failed to do so correctly. This was that (1) in some circumstances it won residents and, possibly, stocks of wealth for the relevant nation which intolerance would have driven away,[11] and (2) benefited the capitalist 'spirit' (however defined) wherever (and of course *only* wherever) it *itself* brought the specific carriers of this spirit to the nation: i.e. wherever it brought people who, *because of their particular religiosity and the particular tie of this religiosity to the 'spirit'*, would not have been tolerated elsewhere. This was precisely the case with ascetic Protestants. And (3), it is nonsense to claim that religious intolerance could have *by itself* uprooted some *non*-religiously grounded 'spirit of capitalism', as Rachfahl feels he has to claim in order to stay 'in the right'. Where has it done that? How could it anyway? And why should it have tried? After all, intolerance permitted the Florentines and all later big capitalists to go about their business in peace, *provided* they showed obedience to the church. Indeed, the church did business *with* them, earning them quite colossal amounts of money. But enough of this.

Since I do not intend to let Rachfahl get away with any significant points if I can help it, sustained as he is by an embarrassing insincerity and – improbable as it may seem – by thoughtless assumptions that rest on *nothing* but distortion, superficial reading or worse, I will now sum up a number of these points and conclude the polemical part of my Reply with just a few more characteristic examples of the things he thinks he can permit himself.[12]

In a great many words as cavilling as they are trivial, Rachfahl tries to convince his readers (*despite* first disowning this intention, and then forgetting his denial in the next column, like his quotations from my essay) that I either *denied* the importance of those features of the capitalist spirit that have *always* accompanied capitalist behaviour or else *only* spoke of the capitalist spirit where ascetic features were present – the features I described as present at the birth of *modern* capitalism.[13] I have already made clear to Rachfahl in my last Reply that this is not correct, that I delimited my task in my essay exactly as indicated in my Reply. However, although even he can now no longer dispute this fact, the way he lets his readers hear of this is that *I now* concede – obviously as a result of his critique! – that the component I analysed 'is not sufficient to explain the modern capitalist system (sic) by a long chalk'. As if, in view of the passages from my essay cited above, this was not already a bit rich, he even asserts in the next sentence that I 'conceded' that my 'capitalist spirit' '*does not at all refer* to large-scale capitalist development'. *Readers* of my essay, for whom his 'critique' and 'reply' are certainly not intended, will recall that what I really said is that precisely that type of amassing of wealth which was conditioned by specifically 'ascetic' conduct of life was what again and again tended to break the power of asceticism – as the recurrent monastic 'Reformations' of the Middle Ages show (to which I referred as parallels), and as the Puritans, Quakers, Baptists, Mennonites and Pietists well knew from their own all-too-understandable experiences. It would become ever rarer for the self-made man[ix] – and certainly for his sons and grandsons – spontaneously to resist the 'temptation' of living for the 'world' (i.e. for the *pleasurable consumption* of acquired goods) – rarer even than for the enriched monasteries of the Middle Ages. In fact, one of the achievements of ascetic Protestantism was that it *combated* this tendency, that it steadily opposed such tendencies to 'idolatry of the flesh' as the securing of 'splendor familiae' through the tying up of one's fortune in real estate as rentier income, along with the 'seigneurial' pleasures of the 'high life',[x] intoxication with beauty and aesthetic enjoyment, excess, pomp and circumstance. And it is these tendencies, so anathema to ascetic Protestantism, which continually evoked the danger of 'capitalist tranquilisation' based on the use of assets for purposes *other* than 'active capital' [*'Erwerbskapital'*] and which thus worked against the capitalist 'spirit' (in *every* sense one can connect with this term). For wherever we find them in big entrepreneurs, each one of these traits hinders the capitalist's full development and undermines 'capitalist accumulation'. And these traits are at the same time precisely those found usually among *all* types of owners of large assets or incomes: among feudal rentiers, coupon issuers and high-salaried state and court officials just *as much* as the big capitalists. However, if the big capitalists at all wished to *remain* capitalists, in the precise sense of being oriented to economic gain [*im präzisen erwerbswirtschaftlichen Sinn*], we necessarily find fewer of these traits among them than the others. For with the growth of 'unproductive' (as one says in today's vague language) uses of their capital and its fertility, their assets are actually *robbed*.

On the other hand, when we consider what private–capitalistic motives remain among those big capitalists who have *not* experienced the power of ascetic methodical life practices, and hence in particular what remains among such men of that conscious planned striving toward extension of one's economic sphere and toward 'accomplishing something in the world' with one's economic powers, we find that the lifestyle that is emancipated from all religious grounding still *shares* with the lifestyle I analysed this striving for gain and acquisition according to definite use of means. However, what it lacks is just some decisive *foundation* in *personal* life. For the optimism that became common after the Enlightenment and

---

[ix]   English in original.
[x]   English in original.

later peaked in 'liberalism' was only a surrogate for the *social* aspect [of ascetic Protestantism]: it replaced the *'in majorem Dei gloriam'*. It could not replace the *personal* significance of 'proof' [of election], which when re-oriented to this world tended rather to flip over into the merely 'agonistic' or to become part of trivial–bourgeois complacency. All those specific features that characterise a life thoroughly imbued with whatever it is that we understand by the 'spirit' of capitalism – whether cool and dispassionate 'objectivity', 'calculativeness', rational consistency, seriousness of work stripped of all naivety, expert specialisation – all these features which have provoked and continue to provoke emotional anti-chrematistic[xi] protest from artistic, ethical and above all purely humanistic points of view, lack any integral unity of ethical justification, even among those committed to them seriously. Rather, as I have indicated already, such unity is replaced, if at all, by all kinds of surrogates easily recognisable as such. Capitalism *can* of course exist very comfortably in this situation, but only either – as increasingly today – as a fatalistically accepted inevitability, or – as in the Enlightenment period and modern-style liberalism – legitimated as a somehow *relatively* optimal means of making the *relative* best of the *relative* best of worlds (so to speak, in the sense of Leibnizian theodicy). It does *not* easily appear – precisely to the most serious people – as the outward expression of a life-style rooted in an ultimate, integral and identifiable wholeness of personality. And it would be a serious mistake to believe that this circumstance remains irrelevant to the position of capitalism in civilisation as a whole, including first its cultural *effects* but equally its inner essence and finally its destiny.

What I said about features of the 'capitalist spirit' *not* conditioned by Protestant asceticism was therefore not such Rachfahlian nonsense as that the big capitalists 'do not belong in modern economic history', but: (1) that even in the Reformation period the ascetic features of the capitalist vocational ethic are far less *specific* to economic 'supermen' (I shall retain this expression for brevity's sake) than to the rising bourgeois middle classes at that time and therefore can be far less studied in them. Quite apart from the already mentioned 'temptations' to which such 'supermen' are especially prone, this of course can be explained simply from, among other things,[14] the fact that people who once find themselves in this position of power, equipped with the possibility of a political and aesthetic horizon, are *much more easily able to bear* the inner situation of the 'Beyond Good

---

[xi] *Anti-chrematistisch*: opposed to the desire for money, from the Greek for 'money', χρῆμα. Aristotle opposed 'chrematism' in favour of 'economy' because the former bred the desire to profit from exchange, whereas the latter only served the needs of subsistence. This became the foundation of medieval teaching on usury. Weber's reference here is probably to the *Kosmiker*, the Stefan George circle.

and Evil,[xii] of being torn loose from ethical and religious ties of conscience, than the bourgeoisie. All historical experience shows this to be so at that time when the bourgeoisie was embarking on its mighty awakening in the modern associations of states, *if* it was to grow inwardly into the 'spirit' of capitalism and mould its lifestyle accordingly. Further, (2) I said that the mere *'auri sacra fames'*, the lust for money, has not only been present in all ages but also is not even typical of the 'capitalist class' in any way; it has been, and still is today, at least as widespread outside as inside it. The oriental small shopkeeper, the barcaiuolo,[xiii] coachman, waiter, porter in present-day Italy and other countries (with the important exception of just those countries influenced by Puritanism), and equally the 'needy yeoman' [*notleidende Agrarier*] – all show even *more* of this lust than the 'capitalist', for if the capitalist is to succeed *in the long run*, he always tends to be characterised by at least a streak of (i) dedication to the 'matter' [*Hingabe an die 'Sache'*] and (ii) rational self-control. The achievement of 'inner-worldly asceticism' was to create unitary *fundamental motives* for cultivating *these* qualities.

Rachfahl answers my reference to his ignorant vulgarisation of the problems at issue by claiming, with typically impudent self-confidence, that 'the weaknesses of the psychological position (sic) of the *acquisitive drive*' are 'well-known' to him. If I may say so, he knew *absolutely nothing* of this, for otherwise he would not have invoked the force of just this 'drive' (among people *other* than Puritans) in that broad and shallow way I rebutted. But 'he knows better' – despite and even because of this. He has now grasped something of my argument from my Reply and from what, on reasonably careful reading, he could find laid out at length in my essay – but not enough to stop him *still* reciting just the same platitudes at numerous points in his own reply. He is quite content to carry on with his 'precocious' tale about the elevation of the acquisitive 'drive' out of the realm of 'naive urges' to the level of the 'rational' being by no means 'solely' the work of the *'Reformed* vocational ethic' (to which I by no means restricted myself, as is well known!), and gives no further clarification of his meaning, nor any supporting reference.[15]

Of a similar standard is Rachfahl's parallel discussion of what I have called the 'ascetic saving compulsion' (*asketischer Sparzwang*). The ethical inculcation of this [into the individual] through inner-worldly asceticism forms the negative complement to that rationalisation and ethical transfiguration of the will to profit that is one's calling. Rachfahl now discovers the astonishing truth that capital accumulation, and therefore *saving*, is characterised by the 'spirit of thrift'. (And incidentally, every novice in political economy knows that capital accumulation

---

[xii]   A reference to Friedrich Nietzsche's *Jenseits von Gut und Böse* of 1886.
[xiii]   Boatmen, ferrymen.

is by no means identical to the amassing of large 'fortunes' of which he speaks, though plainly this is scarcely evident to him.) Since people at all times have had to 'save' in order to accumulate capital, inner-worldly asceticism is evidently nothing 'new', even in its function described here; it mimics the 'acquisitive drive', which likewise has been present in all ages (and therefore had no need at all for the supporting 'prop' of the vocational ethic). I have nothing more to add to the weight of this argument. That certainly in view of the 'Thou shalt not gather treasures on earth' and therefore the *'Deo placere non potest'* of medieval Catholicism, it was asceticism's unique, even paradoxical achievement to preach *just that* Bible maxim *against* saving and, *at the same time*, through the kind of conduct of life it established, constantly to regenerate those abominated 'treasures' with unprecedented momentum and continuity and to protect them from naive hedonistic consumption (*so long as* its 'spirit' kept the upper hand over 'temptation');[16] in a word, that asceticism was able to *rationalise* and *transfigure* both saving and the uses of what had been saved beyond personal pleasure – these simple but fundamental facts are probably not comprehensible to the author of this rather cack-handed 'historical critique' [*für die etwas 'groben Pfoten', mit welchen diese sogen. 'historische Kritik' hantiert*].

After all this, one can be in no doubt of what to think of Rachfahl's claim to have distinguished in his review 'just like' me 'between the mental impulses at work in capitalism in all ages and the Weberian capitalist spirit' and then to say that the hallmarks of *the* modern capitalist spirit are 'the same as they were at all times'. Or likewise to aver that my features were merely a 'nuance' of the 'spirit' that belongs to the modern age 'too' (sic) (and which other epochs as well?), that in particular the 'input of methodical conduct of life was fairly modest', indeed that for many 'capitalist phenomena' (sic) a role for my motives is 'ruled out' (of course he offers not the slightest indication of *which* phenomena these might be), and then to declare (meaning that I have nothing new to say on this score) that no one disputes an 'inner link between Calvinism and capitalism' (which is to put it too narrowly, as I have said) and now that no one at all doubts the decisive role of Puritanism in American ways of life. Actually, in his 'critique' Rachfahl *did* dispute the role of this last extremely emphatically, so far as the specific significance of the Puritan vocational ethic for business life was concerned; indeed he contests it *even now* – though there he will probably stand alone, despite my express observations in *Christliche Welt*, in the essay[xiv] I have cited dozens of times already but was studiously ignored by Rachfahl then as now.

Exactly the same is true, of course, when, without any trace of justification or even explication of what he means but simply, as always, out of the blue, he

---

assures his audience like an 'expert' that the capitalist was already a 'person with a calling' before the influence of my motives; that no reservations *whatever* about the consumption of goods existed in Calvinist ethics; that the 'ethical understanding of vocation' was 'not just a product of Reformed (sic) morality'; that ascetic objections to consumption are not in any way typical 'of the modern capitalist class', not even in *my* sense, as he deliberately adds; and that 'vocational ethics' existed before the Reformation, 'even with a religious colouring'. I, on the other hand, have (1) demonstrated that the very *word* 'calling' was first a very specific product of Luther's Bible translation, which while stemming from purely religious meanings eventually succumbed to secularisation, and (2) I have repeatedly analysed the differences of the Thomist and Lutheran attitude to what since the Reformation has come to be known as 'calling', over against ascetic Protestantism's attitude – without of course Rachfahl's making even the slightest beginnings of an attempt to unsettle this. Instead he just blithely affirms that for me it was a matter of 'mere assertion'.

Or [the same is true] when he contrives to make what I said about ascetic Protestantism's specific significance in the seventeenth century[17] for the bourgeois middle classes rising at just that time and in *just* those Protestant areas seem as though I had not already said it in precisely this way in my essay more or less word for word, and then tries to put it about that the kind of people I meant by 'bourgeois middle classes' merely included 'cobblers'.[18] With this feat I think I can now close my analysis.

It only remains to note that Rachfahl thinks my writing on the 'spirit of capitalism' and only considering *one* specific 'nuance' of this [spirit] is like the author of a book on horses announcing he wants to deal only with white horses. Let me refer this 'critic', as witty as he is forgetful, to the *title* of my essay: The Protestant Ethic *and* the Spirit of Capitalism. Clearly, I was not concerned with the *totality* of these two – otherwise Rachfahl could have accused me of only discussing white horses again, just for not saying everything about the *ethics* part, e.g. Luther's sexual ethics, and so on. Rather, I was concerned with the *relations between* them. From this it follows logically that all I had to deal with was the causal effect that each side exerted on the other.

In my experience, things usually stand badly with a polemic when in order to keep at least appearing 'in the right', the polemicist is forced to *pretend* to be *even more* stupid than (in the present case) he is.

II

But finally, after so much polemic, enough. I am quite forgetting Rachfahl's exceeding kindness in also offering me good advice on how I could have done better.[xv] For what I should have said is: 'under the influence of the Reformed vocational ethic, a certain variation of the capitalist spirit developed in the course of modernity; I want to establish its origin, its limits of expansion and qualitative character; i.e. I want to determine whether the capitalist spirit which created (sic) our present-day capitalist economic system received from this source certain features that became constitutive of its nature'. In other words, I should have

1 first assumed something Rachfahl himself castigates elsewhere, namely that some 'capitalist spirit' (however defined) created the capitalist economic *system* out of itself *alone* – a purely spiritualist construction I expressly rejected in my essays. Furthermore, if I understand him correctly, I should have

2 *presupposed* something (among other things) that I first wanted to *prove*, namely that the Reformed vocational ethic (let us allow him this '*pars pro toto*') decisively influenced the formation of a 'variation of the capitalist spirit' (this expression too we let pass). And then I should have

3 ascertained the limits of its *expansion* – something I was not at all able to do properly and completely in the original essay, and have not yet been able to in more recent contributions. Then finally

4 I should have addressed the misconstrued question of its 'qualitative character' (see above, no. 1). In doing this, however, I would have

5 framed my problem in a way that simply *did not accord with my intentions*; for what interested me *centrally* was not what nurtured the expanding capitalism but the developing type of *human being* that was created out of the confluence of the religious and economic components. I said this clearly enough at the end of my essay.

However, it is evident now that in order to carry out this programme, as far as it makes sense, I would above all have had to include at the start of my investigation a *definition* of all that the complex concept of 'spirit of capitalism' can entail. For without this, establishing the existence of a 'variation' is not possible. But I have said in my essay why I did not do this and could not do it, if I were not to violate history from the outset. A specifically historical formation like the one we at first represent quite unclearly under that name can only be raised to conceptual clarity – and I note the absence of any attempt to refute these remarks – through synthesis of its individual components, as historical reality presents them to us. We do this in such a way that from the reality of the historically given we select in their sharpest, most consistent form those individual features which we find exerting their effect there in a variously arranged, fractured, more or less

---

[xv] Despite the apparent sincerity of this opening line, the following points are meant entirely sarcastically. Weber now quotes Rachfahl's paraphrase of him in Rachfahl's second essay.

consistent and complete way, more or less mixed with other, heterogeneous features, and combine them according to how they belong together, so producing an 'ideal–typical' concept, a thought-construct, to which the *actual* average contents of historical data *approximate* in very different degrees. In truth, every historian, consciously or (most often) unconsciously, continually employs concepts of *this kind* whenever he employs precise 'concepts' at all. I have spoken about this repeatedly outside my essay, and so far without meeting any opposition (and also, incidentally, without at all imagining that through those methodological attempts this far from simple problem were in any way definitively 'settled' – rather, I have every reason to think very modestly of my labours in this direction so far). Thus in the present case of a very complex historical phenomenon, it was only possible to start from the *concretely given* and gradually attempt to elicit our concept by eliminating what is 'inessential' from it, insofar as such concepts can only be formed through selection and abstraction. I therefore proceeded by first

1 calling to mind examples of the remarkably strong congruence disputed as yet by no one between Protestantism and modern capitalism, and in particular capitalistic choice of occupation and capitalistic success. Then, by way of illustration, I
2 gave some examples of just those ethical life-maxims (Franklin) I see as testiying indubitably to the 'capitalist spirit', posing the question of how they differ from other, particularly medieval, maxims. And then I
3 sought to *illustrate*, again through examples, how these spiritual attitudes relate *causally* to the modern capitalist economic system. This then
4 led me to the idea of the 'calling', along with the unique and long-established elective affinity of Calvinism to capitalism (and also of Quakerism and similar sects), that Gothein in particular has noted. At the same time I
5 sought to demonstrate that our contemporary concept of vocation is in some way *religiously* based.

Then there arose a problem relevant *not* to the whole series of essays as I originally intended them but to the one published at that time [in two parts] in the *Archiv für Sozialwissenschaft* (as indeed I explicitly stated at the end of the first part). This was the problem of how the various shadings of Protestantism relate to the idea of the calling, in its significance for the development of those *ethical* qualities among individuals that influenced their suitability for capitalism. This question of course only made sense if such religiously conditioned ethical qualities existed at all. At the time, I could only explain the *nature* of these qualities generally through examples. Therefore, to supplement what I had already said about the problem, I needed to demonstrate ever more thoroughly *that* such qualities did indeed exist among certain strands of Protestant ethics; *which* qualities these were; what *kinds* of Protestantism these qualities so fostered to such a high degree; and *how* they differed from those qualities of the medieval church and of other varieties of Protestantism that were in part acquired and absorbed and in part just tolerated. In so doing, my actual treatment of the problem had to: (1), as far as was possible for a layman in theology, discover first the theoretical and dogmatic anchorage of the ethic among the various shades of Protestantism, in order to show that not merely secondary things were at issue having nothing to do with religious thought-contents; but also (2) accomplish something *very different* from this, namely elucidate the *practical–psychological* motives for actual ethical *behaviour* contained in each of these unique shades of religiosity. Rachfahl has still not once been able to grasp that these two questions concern *completely different things* (to say nothing of all his other distortions and superficialities). He has not grasped how important and interesting is the question (also from a practical standpoint) of what kind of ethical ideals were contained in the church *doctrines* of Catholicism, Luther, Calvin and others in their various similarities and differences, and of whether, as Rachfahl reports, church theory 'expected' the same kinds of behaviour that ascetic Protestantism cultivated practically and psychologically 'from the Catholic layman as well' (rather than just from monks). But nor has he seen that the answer to this question establishes *absolutely nothing* about whether the religious doctrine in question created in its adherents the *psychological vehicle capable of generating a type of behaviour* germane to that doctrine. (It may instead have created a quite different type of behaviour or perhaps one that pushed the doctrine in particular distinct directions.) As I have said myself, one of course finds conscientious *work* by the layman in the world praised and recommended very regularly in all ages, both among ethical theorists and among preachers in the Middle Ages such as Berthold von Regensburg[xvi] and others (although early Christianity, by contrast, essentially shared antiquity's view of 'work' – as Harnack has indicated in a short essay).[19][xvii] Luther's sayings along the same lines are well known. There has certainly been no lack of teaching outside ascetic Protestantism about the blessing of secular work too. But what use is it if (as in Lutheranism) no *psychological premiums* are placed on these theoretical teachings being practised with methodical consistency? Or if (as in Catholicism) far greater premiums are placed on *quite different* kinds of behaviour? Or if, and

---

[xvi] Berthold von Regensburg (1210–72): also known as Berthold of Ratisbon, a popular Franciscan preacher in thirteenth-century Germany.

[xvii] See Weber's note at *Archiv* (XXI:79, n.15a/PE:262, n.19): 'That the peculiar ethical valuation of labour and its dignity was not originally a Christian idea nor even peculiar to Christianity has recently been strongly emphasised by Harnack (*Mitt. Des Ev.-Soz. Kongr.*, 14. Folge, 1905, Nos. 3,4, p.48)'. Adolf von Harnack (1851–1930): Protestant theologian, professor at Leipzig, Giessen, Marburg and Berlin, president of the Social-Evangelical Congress 1903–11.

moreover, through the form of confession, the individual is vouchsafed a means of spiritually unburdening himself of absolutely all kinds of transgressions against church commands over and over again?[20] In contrast to this, Calvinism and Baptism in their development since the late sixteenth century generated the thought of the necessity of ascetic *proof* – proof in life generally and especially in vocational life – as the subjective guarantee of the *certitudo salutis* (i.e. not as an *actual ground* of salvation but as one of the most important reasons for *knowing* one's salvation) [*nicht als Realgrund, sondern als einer der wichtigsten Erkenntnis-gründe der eigenen Bestimmung zur Seligkeit*] and they thereby created a very specific psychological premium for the ascetic methodical life practices they demanded, one whose effectiveness is not easily surpassed in *this* area.

This was the state of affairs I had to address in my writings, along with the methodical life practices it unleashed. I first had to explain the *characteristic* features of these practices and then their inner consistency and the absolute seamlessness with which they were lived out by every *individual* who grew up in the atmosphere these religious powers created – even if not *consciously*, of course.

That these motives also found powerful supports in the various *social* institutions of the churches and in other institutions influenced by the churches and sects I partly sought to indicate briefly in my *Archiv* essay and partly sought to illuminate more clearly in my outline in *Christliche Welt*. Let me recapitulate here. First, the central cultic act of Communion was very specifically emphasised in 'ascetic' Protestantism. The thought that whoever does not belong to God's invisible church but still takes part in this act 'eats and drinks in his own judgement' contains a pathos whose power today has been almost completely lost, even to most of the 'Christians' among us. However, we can still vividly reconstruct it from the older generation's memories of its youth and from the remnants of ecclesiastical gravitas that we have, as it were, shunted into the corners (at least, as we look back at things today). Ascetic Protestantism lacks (and by no means accidentally!) the institution of confession that afforded the Catholic *relief* from the pressure of such pathos-filled questions as the individual's qualification for election. And here too, as everywhere, the problem of whether one belonged to the qualified was answered for the Protestant, not, as for the medieval Catholic, through an adding up of guilt and merit which would be approximately balanced out and then possibly supplemented with ecclesiastical grace, but, as I showed quite specifically in ascetic Protestantism, through a rigid either–or of the whole *personality*, as manifested in the totality of the individual's ethical conduct of life. As I showed in detail, here alone – and again, infinitely more starkly than in Lutheranism – would the individual be confronted with his God and have to rely solely on himself and his state of grace, which he could only perceive from his *entire* conduct of life. And at the same time, his external structuring of life would be very much more subject to *control by his peers*: through the members of the congregation; whereas in Catholicism and Lutheranism it falls ultimately only to the representative of the 'ministry' to settle with himself and the layman whether the individual is ready for Communion. In Calvinism, the responsibility for 'God's glory' not being dishonoured by the participation of someone patently 'wearing' signs of exclusion from the elect concerns *every member* of the whole congregation – for worship of 'God's glory' provided an unambiguous focus for the whole social life, with a power that was in *this* way quite foreign to the other large churches. It was these same laypeople who brought about the Kuyper schism[xviii] barely a generation ago (Kuyper himself was a lay elder), by demanding that Communion be refused to confirmands whom they believed did not qualify and had had examined by out-of-town preachers. What we see behind this ultimately is protest against the principle that any authority that has no place in the concrete self-correcting *congregation* of communicants should interfere in this question [of qualification] in any way – in a question that affects every single member of the congregation directly. The immense social significance of these ways of thinking was revealed most clearly at that time in the New England churches, where the demand for an *ecclesia pura* and especially for a pure community of communicants directly created genuine 'class differences', along with battles and compromises over the position of the 'would-be Christians' concerning their entitlement to bring children for baptism and stand proxy for them, and such like. If one examines the Protestant church ordinances and examines their development and, wherever possible, their practical implementation and reflects on their consequences, one is struck first by how much of that moral regimentation of life that was once given over to the ecclesiastical courts [*Sendgerichte*] in the Carolingian age, or was in the hands of the municipalities at the end of the Middle Ages, or in the hands of the royal police at the time of the territorial states, is here taken on by the church – in widely differing degrees, of course, and generally much more so in the Calvinist than Lutheran areas (for as I indicated in my essay, express *submission* to church discipline on entry to the congregation was emphasised only *after* Calvin).

But as I also stressed, what was, and still is in its vestiges to the present day, incomparably *more* predominant and effective was that kind of ethical 'training'[xix] that the ascetic *sects* imposed on their members. I recounted something of this from contemporary observations of the United States in my *Christliche Welt* essay. The present process of secularisation in American life and the tremendous immigration of diverse elements will quickly wash away this legacy, and the ruthless 'soul-fishing' in recruitment among the competing denominations will weaken

---

[xviii] See Part III, trans. note xxxiv, p.80, in this volume.
[xix] English in original.

the intensity of their achievements in education. Nonetheless, only a little attention to these things suffices to make us see vividly the former importance of those phenomena from the remnants marking their legacy. I remind the reader of what I said in *Christliche Welt* about the function of the sects in economic life (gradually being replaced today by all kinds of purely secular organisations). I refer especially, for example, among numerous similar experiences, to the motive I was told for a young man's entering a Baptist congregation in North Carolina. This was that he was thinking of opening a bank, while on closer questioning it emerged that this was not so much a matter of his reckoning on Baptist custom in particular as on precisely that of the *non*-sectarians who greatly predominated in that area. The reason for this was that whoever wanted to be accepted for baptism there had to be prepared during his 'catechumenate' for an astonishingly systematic investigation of his conduct by the congregation,[xx] with inquiries into all his earlier places of residence. Questions would be asked such as: ever frequented public houses? Ever drunk liquor? Ever played card games? Ever led an 'unclean life'?[xxi] Profligacy? Cheques not paid promptly? Or other debts? Any signs whatever of unreliability in business? And so on. If he was admitted, his credit-worthiness and qualification for business were thereby guaranteed, and he could then beat off any competitor not so legitimated – while, at the same time, any possible exclusion on bad behaviour meant his social excommunication, as always with the sects.[21] We find the same thing already developed 200 years ago.

Another example: the Quakers have always boasted of creating the 'fixed prices' system, so important to capitalism, in place of oriental haggling. And indeed this is so. Historical research shows that, 200 years ago, the reason given for the flourishing of Quaker retail trading was that customers felt sure of this principle being adhered to, surer than any medieval or modern price regulation could make them. The Quaker congregation also stepped in when anyone began a business transaction for which he lacked the necessary capital or knowledge, or such like. And in the literature of all these sects one finds that soon after their emergence they would rejoice that the Lord was visibly blessing them, that the 'children of the world' were bringing their money to them (as deposit, as investment or in any other form) rather than to members of their own confession or non-members, because the sects would be sure to provide the requisite personal ethical guarantees. I refer to similar examples in my *Christliche Welt* outline. Let me only note further that, as everyone knows, until the last few decades the old-style Yankee – indeed *precisely* the *businessman* – simply could not understand, and sometimes even today cannot understand, that a person should belong to no

---

[xx] Catechumenate: preparatory instruction for baptism.
[xxi] English in original.

'denomination'[xxii] at all (it does not matter which denomination: in this regard he is absolutely 'tolerant'). Any such religious outlaw would have been suspect to him, both socially and in business, *because* not ethically 'legitimated'. Until at most 15 years ago, even the tourist could be reminded of a similar outlook in Scotland and bourgeois English circles, particularly on Sundays. Today, having escaped this once overwhelming necessity for religious legitimation, the businessman of the American middle classes instead has at his disposal various other organisations that are increasingly emerging. He typically supports his legitimation by having himself balloted into them so as to demonstrate certain 'gentlemanly' qualities, and wears their 'badge' in his buttonhole. (If one watches out for them, one sees such insignia on a massive scale, reminiscent of the legion of honour rosette.)

As long as the true Yankee spirit ruled, American democracy was never a simple heap of sand composed of isolated individuals, even disregarding all the trusts and trade unions. To a great degree, it was a jumble of *exclusive* organisations, of which the prototype is the *sect*, and all of them demanded from their members and cultivated in them those qualities that go to make up the kind of business gentleman capitalism requires. Admittedly, someone in the position of Mr Pierpont Morgan[xxiii] has no such need of legitimation to fulfil his economic position. And in other ways too, things are quite different today. But the penetration of that specific 'spirit' that these associations fostered into the whole of life was certainly an extremely important precondition for modern capitalism to 'take root', i.e. for it to discover an adequate 'lifestyle' in the broad stratum of the bourgeois middle classes and finally also in the masses that it had to fit into its mechanisms, and thereby gain the power over life that it did. Understandably, historians of Rachfahl's type have no idea of the scale of socialisation necessary for this to occur.[22] And if anyone with the 'common sense' Rachfahl trumpets so loudly comes to consider it 'plausible' that this qualification of religious training for business life and this whole configuration of specifically business and religious credentials may possibly be a *consequence* of those religious communities developing in an already capitalist 'milieu' – this person I ask: why, then, did the Catholic Church *not* develop such a combination of attitudes and such a system of education so geared towards capitalism? Why did it not do so, either in the great centres of the Middle Ages like Florence where, God knows, capitalism was incomparably more 'developed' than in the still sparsely settled farming area of

---

[xxii] English in original.

[xxiii] John Pierpont Morgan (1837–1913): very powerful US financier and industrialist, reorganised several major US railroads and consolidated the US Steel, International Harvester and General Electric corporations.

western North Carolina I wrote about, or than in the largely subsistence-economy areas of the American colonies where this religious spirit took root well over 200 years ago? And why did Lutheranism not do so either? It was because [in the movements I described] a web of psychic meanings came to be woven out of quite unique moral and religious roots, offering *possibilities* for capitalist development. It is true that the lifestyle cultivated by the ascetic communities with such immense energy also 'rubbed off' onto that of *other competing* denominations in confessionally mixed areas, from the very beginning and increasingly with the ever greater permeation of economic life by the capitalist spirit, despite intense differences between them.[23] This was so very early on for Dutch and American Lutheranism and even American Catholicism (while for German Lutheranism the older Pietism was the conduit, as is well known). Naturally, this process of 'assimilation' only gradually lessened the differences between them and never fully erased them.[24] However, as far as we can tell today, a movement towards the *most consistent* forms of Protestant asceticism (Calvinist in particular) almost always did occur, certainly at least among those groups that contained Protestants mixed in with them, and for that reason alone a mere statistic of true Calvinists among the Protestant emigrants could still be no argument against the significance of the ascetic forms of life. Contemporary discussions in Catholicism over how best to match the Protestants' economic superiority find their counterpart, in content if not style of expression, in some of Spener's remarks on the good progress of the Quakers. This motive has of course always been at work *tacitly* everywhere, just as in America today.

Leaving quite aside for the moment the *term* 'inner-worldly asceticism',[25] if one now asks finally whether I am justified in drawing a *substantive* parallel between this and Catholic monastic asceticism, I have no need to mention that Protestant ethical writers, especially in England, regularly quoted medieval devotional literature of monastic origin (Bonaventura[xxiv] and others) in connection with the requirements I called 'ascetic'. But we can also compare much more simply than this. Monastic asceticism demanded chastity. Protestant asceticism (in my sense of the word) demanded chastity in marriage *as well*, in the sense of the elimination of 'desire' and the restriction of sexual intercourse to the *rational* 'natural purpose' of procreation as its only morally acceptable outlet. At all events, these regulations were more than *mere* theorising. We know of certain Pietistic and Herrnhut rules of this kind, and some strike us as directly unnatural today. On the other hand, attitudes to women in general have seen the *abolition* of the view of them as principally sexual vehicles – in contrast to Luther's residual peasant outlook.

[xxiv] Bonaventura (1221–74): medieval scholastic philosopher noted for his writings on mysticism and for his leading role in the Franciscan order.

Monastic asceticism also demanded poverty – and we know with what paradoxical consequences. Everywhere, the prosperity of the monasteries was viewed as the result of divine blessing – with the exception of certain strictly spiritual denominations that the popes treated with great suspicion – and indeed *was* in the greatest measure the *consequence* of their rational economy, alongside their endowments. Similarly, I have set out the equally paradoxical consequences of the way in which Protestant asceticism for its part rejected both contented 'satisfaction' with one's possessions and the pursuit of them 'for their own sake'. Monastic asceticism demanded independence from the 'world' and condemned naive pleasure in particular. Protestant asceticism did likewise. Both also join up in their use of the *means* of 'exercise' (for this is what the word 'asceticism' means): strictly divided time; work; silence as a means of subduing the instincts; detachment from overly strong bonds to the flesh (dubiousness of overly intensive personal friendships and such like) and the renunciation of pleasure as such, whether 'sensuous' pleasure in the narrowest sense or aesthetic–literary pleasure, and, in general, renunciation of all use of worldly goods not justifiable on *rational* grounds, for example hygiene. I also pointed out at length that in the Middle Ages he who lived 'methodically' specifically because of his *'calling'* was precisely the monk. Sebastian Franck's remark[xxv] (on which Rachfahl now 'founds' my scientific thesis, with his usual sense of honour, even though I first cited it in my Reply as the view of *contemporaries*) therefore shows rather more understanding of these things than my 'critic'. What distinguishes *rational* Protestant asceticism (in *my* sense of the word) from monastic asceticism is:

1 its rejection of all irrational ascetic means (and such means are also, incidentally, similarly rejected or limited by some of the more significant Catholic orders, particularly by the Jesuits);
2 its rejection of contemplation; and finally and most importantly
3 its change of direction towards inner-worldly asceticism, its working out of itself in the family and (ascetically interpreted) vocation, from which result the differences already mentioned and all others.

But if the kinds of 'spirit' in each of these two contrasting principles of life regulation are *not* to be judged as inwardly and essentially parallel and akin to each other [*nicht als im innersten Wesen parallel und miteinander verwandt*], I do not know when one should ever speak of an 'affinity' [*Verwandtschaft*]. As an aside, I will only mention how greatly the disappearance of the monasteries was regretted occasionally in Pietistic circles, along with that of the monastery-like organisations that were constantly recreated by these circles, and I refer further to what I

[xxv] See Part III, trans. note vii, p.63, in this volume.

wrote in my essay about Bunyan, for example. The inner tension and inner affinity between these two formations concerning the place of ascetic ideals in the total system of religious life arise ultimately from the reason already mentioned: from the fact that what for the monks counted as an *actual ground* of candidature for salvation signified for ascetic Protestantism a *cognitive ground* (that is, *a* cognitive ground but not *the* absolute or only ground, though probably the most important one). And as even modern 'methodologists' (specifically historical methodologists) cannot always distinguish these two sets of facts, it is certainly not surprising that this Protestant 'work holiness' often seemed to resemble Catholic elements like one egg to another – except that the seeds [of the eggs] came from different spiritual fathers and therefore developed very different inner structures.

To recapitulate the *dogmatic* foundations of inner-worldly asceticism here would be going too far. I must refer the reader wholly to my essay for this, where I also suggest, at least provisionally and hence very sketchily, that the question of whether these foundations were provided by the Calvinist doctrine of Predestination or by the Baptist movement's untheological dogmatics was not completely irrelevant to practical life orientation, despite all assimilation between them. But these in many ways very marked differences between them necessarily came second in this part of my project (the only part published so far) to what was common between them. It would be too much to go into detail here. Nonetheless, I must expressly reiterate that in empirically re-examining the question of whether those fundamental religious–psychological conditions had the specific effect on the *practice* of life I claimed they did, I adduced not textbooks of dogma or theoretical treatises on ethics but quite different sources. The publications I singled out by Baxter and Spener in particular rested on pastoral work, essentially on answers to the inquiries of pastors on matters of concrete practical life. To the extent that they reflected *practical* life, these writings therefore represent a genre rather like the *responsa* of the Roman jurists to matters of appropriate practice in business and the law courts. Like the Roman jurists, these and similar works certainly also contained casuistic speculations, as did the Talmud – albeit on an enormous scale quite incomparable with the former – which likewise borrowed from once directly practical responses to problems. The form and context of these writings indicate where they draw from life – not always, of course, but fortunately often enough. And where they do so, *no* source matches them in authenticity and liveliness, except letters and, at best, autobiographies. Neither popular pamphlets and tracts nor sermons match them (though one may rightly use these last extensively *as a supplement* of course), nor any other literary products of the period (however important as a secondary source), nor finally even the quite superficial statements of confessional belonging of the various capitalist groups – especially if one leaves out of the picture the influence of the Protestant ascetic 'atmosphere of life' on them. We are unfortunately very seldom lucky enough to see the meshing together of religious and capitalist interests in the workplace so clearly as in the case of the Kidderminster weavers I cited.[xxvi]

This is not to belittle in the slightest the importance of the works Rachfahl wishes to see. *But* only my approach is capable of disclosing the *specific direction* in which a particular colour of religiosity was able to develop – and this was what explicitly concerned me. This course of influence did not merely 'intensify' some already present psychological outlook; it signified a *new 'spirit'*, at least within the worldly sphere. From their religious lives, their religiously conditioned family traditions and religiously influenced lifestyle and surrounding world, these people developed a habitus that made them uniquely suited to meet the demands of early modern capitalism. In a nutshell, in the shoes of the entrepreneur whose 'chrematism'[xxvii] made him feel *at most* 'tolerated' by God, who like the native Indian trader today had to work off or make up for his *'usuraria pravitas'*, entered a new kind of entrepreneur who kept his good conscience intact. The new entrepreneur was filled with a consciousness that Providence was showing him the path to profit not unintentionally, that he might tread this to the glory of God, that God was visibly blessing him in the increase of his profit and property, and that above all, as long as he achieved it by legal means, he could measure his worth by success in his calling – not only before men but before God – and finally that God had his purposes in selecting *him* for economic ascent and equipping him with the necessary means – unlike the others destined to poverty and hard labour, for good but unfathomable reasons. This was the kind of entrepreneur who would make his way in 'Pharisaic' certainty according to strict formal legality; for this he saw as the highest and only tangible virtue (since there was no such thing for him as 'adequacy' before God). Alongside him stood the man of specific 'readiness for work', in the person of the cottage-industry craftsman or worker, whose conscientiousness in his divinely willed 'calling' made him conscious of his religious state of grace. These men's condemnation of the sin of idolatry of the flesh in sitting on one's laurels, enjoying pleasures and squandering money and time on things not useful for one's calling constantly drove them to make use of property acquired in their calling along the 'vocational' path of capital investment (in the entrepreneur's case) or to pursue the course of 'saving' and thereby possibly rising in the world (in the case of the 'ethically' qualified propertyless).

[xxvi] Weber is referring to his citation of Richard Baxter's remarks on the 'civility' and 'piety' of the hand-loom weavers at Kidderminster in his autobiography. See *Archiv* (XXI:56, n.113/PE:250, n.152) and (XXI:78, n.14/PE:262, n.17).

[xxvii] See trans. note xi, p.102, in this volume.

What was decisive here was that vocation and innermost ethical core of personality remained in unbroken unity. However many isolated moves toward a practical vocational ethic one may find in the Middle Ages (and I have deliberately avoided speaking about this here)[26] do not alter the fact that a 'spiritual linkage' of this kind was simply *lacking* at that time. And in our times today, which place such specific *value* on 'life' and 'lived experience', and such like, an *inner dissolution* of this unity and an ostracising of the 'vocational man' are as plain as can be. For a long time now, modern capitalism has no longer needed this prop – and it is against this hurly-burly [*Getriebe*] of modern capitalism that the modern sensibility I have just mentioned rebels, not only on social–political grounds but now precisely on account of its bondage to the 'spirit' of vocational humanity. Admittedly, we do still find traces of a role for religious contents in capitalist development, as I repeatedly showed in my essay and elsewhere. We can see where industry continues to rely on those qualities of its personnel that arose out of this lifestyle often enough in the distribution of confessions across upwardly mobile foremen and white-collar workers, in contrast to ordinary workers, and likewise among entrepreneurs.[xxviii] Statistics will of course only reveal this for us once we have eliminated those contingencies that enter in through location (such as the presence of essential raw materials in a certain area) and through the inclusion of craftwork trades in the statistics. But on the whole, contemporary capitalism is, I repeat, most definitely and extensively emancipated from such moments. In the period of early modern capitalism, by contrast, no one has so far thought to *doubt* that the Huguenots were linked to French bourgeois capitalism extremely closely and exported their typical commercial qualities *wherever* they emigrated in the late seventeenth century (after the revocation of the Edict of Nantes).[xxix] They did so *not* only to countries with less-developed economies but also, *of all places*, to Holland where capital investment, as I have remarked already, was in part differently structured and in part tranquillised by rentier expenditure and social ostentation, albeit only in certain strata. In his review (though not now in his reply), Rachfahl denies that in the northern states of the US bourgeois–capitalist development rested in a quite *specific* way on the likewise quite specifically conditioned Puritan lifestyle there, though he does admit such a link for England (albeit in his usual vague way). The English Romantics recognised just this correlation in Scotland,[27] and, in Germany, Gothein[xxx] has already ascertained these things, with a few examples added by me. I have offered reasons why ascetic Protestant forces in Holland

---

[xxviii] This is probably a reference to the Oerlinghausen linen factory, which also figures in the study on industrial psychology (Weber 1908b).

[xxix] See trans. note vi, p.99, in this volume.

[xxx] See trans. note xxxix, p.122, in this volume.

working in *just the same* direction were in some degree crushed,[28] in keeping with the remarkable stagnation that set in to Holland's capitalist expansion fairly soon afterward (and not necessarily just its colonial expansion).[29] This was due to a tangle of causes partly mentioned already, of which I scarcely dare claim to have noted even the most important so far. Just as with the economic life of certain medieval sects, all this has been known about largely since the seventeenth century, and so far no one who has taken any interest in the issue has doubted it. It is in fact *impossible* to contest, certainly least of all (for the reasons already given) by observations such as that in Frankfurt, Dutch Lutheran immigrants existed alongside the Dutch Calvinist immigrants – however historically valuable these observations may be in themselves. I therefore merely *reminded* readers of these things in my essay. I now also *remind* them again that the many (though not *all*) Russian schismatics and sectarians who held an essentially ascetic–*rational* outlook showed quite similar economic behaviour, as soon as they had outgrown their youthful otherworldly period. Here the most extreme combination of business acumen with ethical 'world-rejection' was shown by the eunuch sect.[xxxi]

My essay had to rest content with *illustrations* of things well-known already (and must still do so here, despite Rachfahl's quibbling). Further research into the power of the various confessions was not my concern, useful and necessary as it may be for specialised historical analysis of particular regions. However necessary (indeed substantially *more necessary*) it may be to *compare* the various characteristics of the individual countries influenced by ascetic Protestantism (which alone will help explain evident differences in development), the most pressing questions for me lay and lie elsewhere. First, of course, I needed to differentiate the various effects of Calvinist, Baptist and Pietist ethics on lifestyle, much more deeply and in detail than had been done before. We must also investigate thoroughly the beginnings of similar developments in the Middle Ages and early Christianity, as far as Troeltsch's works still leave scope for this – which will certainly require very intensive collaboration with theologians.[30] Then we need to consider how best to explain, from the *economic* standpoint, that ubiquitous elective affinity of the bourgeoisie to a definite kind of lifestyle, showing up as it does always in different manifestations and yet always with a similar common root; and in particular, we need to study that specific affinity of the bourgeoisie to certain aspects of the religious lifestyle, the aspects that were most consistently exemplified by ascetic Protestantism. Numerous things have been said from many different quarters about this more general problem, but much more remains to be said – including, I believe, all that is fundamental.

[xxxi] A reference to the Skoptsy, a castration sect dating from the 1770s.

There is one question in particular Rachfahl fiddles about with in the most desperate way: that of *which* agencies in the overall picture of modern capitalism definitely ought *not* be understood in terms of 'inner-worldly asceticism'. My brief answer to this is: the 'adventurers' of capitalist development – taking the concept of 'adventurer' in the sense given it recently by G. Simmel in a delightful short essay.[xxxii] As is well-known, the economic significance of adventurers in history was very considerable, especially in the early capitalist period (and not only then). But one can also, in a certain sense and with a pinch of salt, see capitalism's increasing domination over all economic life in terms of the transformation of *economic opportunism into an economic system*. Thus the genesis of the capitalist 'spirit' in my sense of the word could be understood in terms of the transformation of the *romanticism of economic adventurism into the economic rationalism of methodical life practices.*[31]

And finally if anyone wanted to know my view of capitalism's probable fate (as an economic *system*) if we *imagined* the specifically modern elements of the capitalist 'spirit' *not* having unfolded as they have – and it will be recalled that Rachfahl dropped what I believe are some quite thoughtless remarks on this question – all one can honestly answer is that, in short, we do not know. However, those people – those non-specialists, at least – who cannot disabuse themselves of the myth that certain *technological* 'achievements' were the clear cause of capitalist development ought to be reminded of the broad features of this legacy. Ancient capitalism unfolded *in the absence* of technical 'progress', indeed almost at the very moment technological advances were coming to an end. Technological advances in medieval continental Europe were not insignificant for the *possibility* of capitalist modernisation, but were certainly no decisive 'catalyst'. Objective factors such as certain climatic variables influencing conduct of life and labour costs were important historical preconditions, along with other factors generated by the social–political organisation of medieval society with its largely *inland culture* (in comparison with antiquity) and by the resultant unique character of the medieval city, especially the inland city, and its *burghers* (see my article in the *Handwörterbuch der Staatswissenschaften*).[xxxiii] An additional and specifically economic moment were certain new forms of trading organisation (the cottage industries) which, compared with antiquity, were perhaps not absolutely new but were certainly new in structure, distribution and significance. The great process of development that *spans* the then still highly *fragile* career of capitalism in the late Middle Ages and the technological *mechanisation* so decisive for capitalism today has been fulfilled by certain important objective–political and objective–economic *preconditions*.

[xxxii] Simmel 1911.
[xxxiii] Weber 1909.

Above all, however, it has been fulfilled by the birth and nurturing of that ratio-nalistic and anti-traditionalistic 'spirit' and by the rise of that whole type of human being that practically carried it forward of which I have spoken. We must look, on the one hand, to the history of modern *science* and its practical effects on modern economic life, and, on the other, to the history of modern *conduct of life*, again in its practical economic significance. I discussed the latter in my essay, and it is worth further discussion. But the development of rational methodical *practices* in conduct of *life* is clearly something fundamentally different from *scientific* ratio-nalism, and by no means simply given with the latter. The first touchstones of modern natural science sprang up in *Catholic* areas and in Catholic heads. What was principally 'Protestant' was rather the methodical application of science to *practical* purposes, just as were certain specific principles of *methodical life* and the kind of affinity they seem to have shown to Protestant ways of thinking – but more detail on this here would lead too far afield. The error of regarding 'devotion', how-ever strict, as an *intrinsic* obstacle to the development of *empirical* sciences at that time and later is proved in particular by most of the English heroes of the natural sciences from the seventeenth century to Faraday and Maxwell (indeed Faraday is still known to have *preached* in his sect's church in the nineteenth century).[xxxiv] The *practical* and *methodical*, and not just occasional, enlisting of the natural sciences in the service of the economy has been a keystone for the rise of 'methodical life' in *general*, and to this must be added the decisive contributions of both the Renais-sance and the Reformation, particularly in the direction I adumbrated. If I am now asked in all honesty how *high* I rate the importance of the Reformation, my answer is that I rate it *very* highly indeed. I have constantly and scrupulously reflected on this question, and am not bothered that no 'numerical' ratio exists for historical attribution here.

Enough and more than enough. I think I have at least proved that my 'critic' belongs to just that type of wrangler [*Klopffechter*] who always only remains right before a mass of readers who cannot really be expected to have read the text in question – for what they will have read first is so utterly devoid of understanding and dishonourable in content. That a history professor with such self-confidence should have fundamentally misunderstood the whole *question* at issue on account of extremely superficial reading and *parti pris*, and then not summoned up the necessary qualities to *admit* this when pointed out to him – this will surely be dif-ficult to believe for people not familiar with the subject. Such incredulity notwithstanding, however, this *is*, unfortunately, *the case*, as I have been able to

---

[xxxiv] Faraday and his parents belonged to a small and isolated sect known as the Sandemanians, after Robert Sandeman. Faraday attended meetings of the sect from childhood and made public pro-fession of his faith at the age of 30. During two different periods he discharged the office of elder.

demonstrate[32] – albeit at the cost of journal space which cannot stand ready and waiting in such abundance for such inevitably *sterile* polemic, brought on solely by the 'critic', as apparently it can in the *Internationale Wochenschrift*.

Weber's Notes

1   Let me stress that the absolute worthlessness of Rachfahl's 'critical' achievements does not in the least affect my high regard for other works of his which do not venture into areas unfavourable to him. However, I say 'unfavourable' here, not only because he is ill-informed of the *subject-matter* but also because his pleasure in learned 'duelling' for its own sake constantly threatens to get carried away into 'below-the-belt' [*incommentmäßige*] strikes ('swine'-strikes [*'Sau'-Hieben*], as we used to call them in the student argot). Indeed, this duelling pleasure of his typically becomes so rampant and unbridled as to constantly fall short of its 'object'. He censures the inconsiderate form of my reply to him; and yet the intentionally generous and accommodating way Troeltsch engaged with him – in both form and content – has resulted only in his seeking 'tactically' to exploit this generosity in a way that is scarcely honourable; and his sallies against Troeltsch carry a degree of animosity that outdoes even that directed towards me. The way he 'criticises' inevitably becomes sheer wrangling [*Klopffechten*], so that one cannot help but speak bluntly with someone like this. I hope I shall never have to settle with a 'critic' like this again. A more honourable kind of polemic, even a formally quite caustic one, would have raised very different considerations for me, and even were I obliged to contest its contents no less caustically, I could scarcely have been led to take such a dim view of it. What other impression can I be expected to have of a 'critic' who, *without showing the slightest competences* in the matter, sees fit to begin his 'debate' with me by asserting that I made my task too 'easy' for myself and then ends by warning people to take care with 'the Weberian discoveries'?

2   In order to dispel all doubt concerning whom I meant by those 'others' whose appropriation of my work I found in places one-sided, let me say that I think Hans Delbrück[xxxv] in particular has been trumpeting far too much about some historians still being intent on 'refutations' of the materialist view of history. However carefully put together, I can only accept F.J. Schmidt's intellectual constructions *as* 'constructions' (also in the *Preußische Jahrbücher*). Without meaning thereby to devalue them in themselves, it seems to me they too conclude too much from what I have only so far been able to show in any detail. My friend von Schulze-Gaevernitz's[xxxvi] 'British imperialism' is a very far from simple construct – still less one based solely on my ideas, as Rachfahl assumes. If this writer has utilised my ideas at all, he has very happily supplemented and expanded them. Indeed he will not deny that he concentrates quite 'one-sidedly' on the intellectual direction of causation: this is both his strength and, if you will, his weakness. I completely agree of course with Bonn[xxxvii] that a dualism runs throughout English history of the last 300 years between the squirearchy and those bourgeois middle classes who characteristically inclined towards dissent, right up until Cobden's movement.[xxxviii] But Schulze-Gaevernitz will not dispute this.

Exaggerations such as those of Delbrück were not helpful to the purpose of my essay, which dealt with a clearly defined subject and, if I may say so, did so with plain and unpretentious objectivity. Having explicitly recorded my objections to these, I cannot be held responsible for them, and I took the first opportunity to do what I could to prevent them

[xxxv] Hans Delbrück (1848–1929): professor of history at Berlin and editor of the *Preußische Jahrbücher*.

[xxxvi] Gerhart von Schulze-Gaevernitz (1864–1943): professor of economics at Freiburg from 1893–1926.

[xxxvii] A reference to an article by M.J. Bonn in the *Frankfurter Zeitung*. See PE:217, n.31.

– as Rachfahl *well knew*, since he cites the discussion in question. I therefore scarcely needed Rachfahl's subsequent kind assistance. If he carries on playing off such exaggerations against *me*, let him settle this with his literary conscience.

To say something about Troeltsch's account of my views would of course be out of place here, and so would anything on von Schubert's brief comment. But in Troeltsch's case, only *a few sentences* were *sufficient* to lead Rachfahl to try to fructify his position by zealously wringing them dry like the Talmudic exegesis of passages from the Torah (which he now declares the essence of 'historical criticism'!). As for Gothein,[xxxix] Rachfahl either does not know or has simply forgotten (despite the reference in my essay) that this gentleman's remarks on the subject were printed over a decade *before my essay was published*. Gothein of course has not altered his position. Where I believe I truly differ from writers whose findings touch on mine, I am not in the habit of keeping quiet about. So now Rachfahl's boldly self-assured manner has given Troeltsch the impression that I only belatedly 'brought in' something to substantiate my views – much to Rachfahl's delight, who of course as usual henceforth only invokes *Troeltsch* as the authority on what I said. I can only ask yet again that people read my essay and see for themselves that *everything* I said in my Reply appeared just as clearly in my essay. The *only* points I introduced in my Reply were two details answering Rachfahl's objection about Hamburg and capitalist development in Holland, along with my reference to conditions in the Wupper valley (and I could have also discussed Calw[xl] and Pietism here). Indeed I mentioned these things despite not considering them necessary since Gothein has already demonstrated the specific importance of Calvinism for Germany. That is all! But of what consequence are these tiny 'additions' in comparison with what I showed in my essay for *all* the major regions of ascetic Protestantism – in England, France, the Netherlands, America?

It goes without saying that Troeltsch did not re-examine *my* essay from to A to Z in a controversy about *his* theories, since he was solely answering for himself and had only mentioned me in passing. Troeltsch thought Rachfahl at least partly reliable. But can we think that of this person who claims to have thoroughly 'criticised' my essays, and moreover with a supposed 'exactitude' of 'historical criticism' he thinks Troeltsch cannot match?

Particularly characteristic is the passage where Rachfahl tells his readers (in the spaced type he likes for the individual *words* he fixes on) that because I speak of ascetic Protestantism also creating capitalism's corresponding 'soul', the soul of the 'vocational man', (where of course the context makes clear that I mean the specifically *bourgeois*–capitalist development of my period), the 'habitus' I analysed therefore itself contains *all* the motives operating in *contemporary* capitalism. (And then the one exception he kindly grants me to this rule is capitalism of Jewish origin – just because in a *completely different* place and in just *one or two words* I mentioned the importance of the treatment of Jews by states, as a case where tolerance or intolerance could indeed become economically relevant. See below.) Most pitiful of all in this hair-splitting is when Rachfahl says he finds it 'at least excusable' that others have 'absolutised' this one motive of mine (from the words he picked out), naming Troeltsch, von Schubert and Gothein (despite Gothein's work appearing over a

---

[xxxviii] Richard Cobden (1804–65): English radical MP, leader of the Anti-Corn Law League which successfully campaigned for the repeal of the Corn Laws in 1846 on the grounds that tax on imported grain raised the domestic price of food and was both economically disastrous and morally wrong. Cobden himself belonged to the Church of England but found support among religious dissenters of the middle classes.

[xxxix] Eberhard Gothein (1853–1923): historian, economist and political scientist, professor at Karlsruhe, Bonn and Heidelberg. See Part I, trans. note xvii, p.37, in this volume.

[xl] Predominantly Protestant town and surrounding region in the north-east Black Forest, notable for its tradition of handicraft and skilled light industry besides forestry.

decade earlier, as I said) – and this after assuring us that he himself made no such mistake, when we have seen he made it in his review and occasionally *still* does so. Actually, I find this all rather second-rate. In what tones should one answer a 'critic' who speaks of my venturing in my Reply to solve questions I had never before 'tackled'?

3   Even this formulation is really too naive for a historian. Whether something 'goes beyond the religious domain' is *precisely* the point of contention on which hinges every *Kulturkampf* in history until today. Rachfahl claims *he* would not find it difficult to draw the boundary. That he nonetheless makes no attempt to do so seems to me no loss; for he then expresses the curious view that 'actors in history often showed a remarkably fine instinct' for this. Well, it was this 'fine instinct' that made it permissible for some Huguenot army commanders to indulge in piracy – and the same instinct that led both Huguenot merchants and members of the Huguenot synods (who had no economic interests but still remained historical 'actors') to try to call them to account for it. The same 'instinct' led the Stuarts to fight the Puritans' ascetic day of rest on Sundays, and the radical Puritans to fight the tithes on which the universities depended, which in turn led Cromwell to break with the radical Puritans. The same supposedly clear instinct inspired Bismarck's May Laws and the papacy's rulings on Catholic political behaviour in Italy and Germany, and finally also the opposition of the [Prussian] Centre Party to both the May Laws and (occasionally) the papacy.[xli] All the difficulties that Vatican dogma faces and will face, and all the difficulties of separating church from state, result from the *inherent* impossibility of drawing a clear boundary to what is relevant to religion. Thus the idea that only 'modern theologians' could be in any doubt about such a boundary belongs in the political kindergarten. These points are common knowledge; it never occurred to me to pass them off as my own, as Rachfahl spitefully makes out. So even if I was not truly of the view that 'whole generations of historians' need to go on pursuing these matters to the point of exhaustion (since no historian committed to serious objective discussion could forget them in the way Rachfahl does for the sake of staying in the right), I still believe Rachfahl and his like need to be firmly reminded of them.

Rachfahl made it his special task to oppose a putative 'Heidelberg' specialism. I read a dissertation by a doctoral student of his which deals among other things with G. Jellinek's[xlii] work on the role of religion in the rise of 'human rights'. I saw how it reported the views it attacks and hunted out alleged 'contradictions' and so on in just the same way as its master's 'critical' manner. Clearly, no one is inclined or obliged to take responsibility for everything in a doctoral dissertation – I certainly would not. But in this case the candidate's '*manner*' is hardly coincidental.

When Rachfahl sums up his view of the development of American democracy by asserting, against Troeltsch, that it 'essentially *developed by itself*', this original solution might certainly have the advantage of a recommendable simplicity for all historical questions. But seriously, the fact that the religious basis of life was completely *taken for granted* in the formally strictly neutral American nation was precisely what most *distinguished* it from the European and other democracies. And as Troeltsch admirably brought out, it was also

---

[xli]   As part of his strategic assault on the growing power of the opposing Roman Catholic Centre Party in the Prussian parliament, whom he saw as undermining the integrity of the mainly Protestant German *Reich*, Bismarck and his minister of education, Adalbert Falk, introduced a series of laws in May 1873 which controlled the education of the clergy through a state examination and provided for a state veto on clerical appointments. Fierce Catholic resistance with support from Pope Pius IX led to further retaliation with the dismissal, fining or imprisonment of numerous bishops and a law dissolving all Catholic monastic foundations in 1875. These laws were eventually repealed in 1887. This conflict of the Prussian state with the Catholic church was known as the *Kulturkampf*.

[xlii]   Georg Jellinek (1851–1911): professor of law at Basel and Heidelberg.

what gave the 'separation of state and church' such a completely different cachet over there. One can quite seriously question whether *without* this basis and its taken-for-granted character in *all* areas of life (which I too illustrated in *Christliche Welt*), American democracy would have been possible in its original unique form. Today all this is fading away, and the prayer that opens the supreme court of justice and every *party assembly*, together with the 'chapel record' (sic) mentioned in the statutes of numerous universities as a requirement for the semester to be counted, have of course become a farce, like our service at the opening of the Reichstag. But things were once very different!

4   Troeltsch says (and Rachfahl quotes this) that with his examples Rachfahl sought 'to illustrate the ineffectiveness of the religious factor in life in general'.

5   Rachfahl himself indicates that he has been confused by my explanations. I need take no responsibility for this, as his review and reply will show anyone who wishes to see.

6   Just so that no doubt remains here either: what Rachfahl exploits are trivia such as Troeltsch's errors about my relationship to Sombart and about what I said in my essay about members of the Reformed church in Hungary and the like – things he now still dishes up to his audience even after my pointing out the error of his reliance on Troeltsch. And amusingly, this has not prevented his telling Troeltsch, who rightly remains heartily indifferent to all this, that in view of such sins historical criticism 'will not have the courage to soar to this lofty and pleasant standpoint' (sic).

7   Rachfahl writes: 'Here we arrive at Troeltsch's and Weber's *fundamental* difference ... in their conception (sic) of early Protestant asceticism'. This is supposedly due to my accepting *'no* idea of a generic Protestant ethic (sic) [*gesamtprotestantische Ethik*] in Troeltsch's sense' (sic). Compare this with Rachfahl's talk of the 'Weber–Troeltsch' concept of asceticism (and now even of 'the Weber–Troeltsch hypothesis') and with his assertion that what I say about 'ascetic lifestyle' 'comes to the same thing' as Troeltsch's 'definition' of asceticism. Rachfahl's whole tirade against Troeltsch and me shows how he has only created this 'question' for the sake of polemic.

8   What I can only call his little wrangler's dodge [*Klopffechterkunstgriff*] is entirely indicative here when he makes out a 'contradiction' between, on the one hand, Troeltsch's saying he merely 'adopted' my conclusions where they *supplemented* his – and therefore meaning obviously that he merely *reported* them, by reviewing and agreeing with them – and, on the other hand, my saying that there had been no 'adoption' of my theories by Troeltsch – and thereby meaning obviously in terms of a scientific *foundation* for his own very different research. Now Rachfahl even tries to convince his readers that Troeltsch's works are 'the one coherent attempt to show how Weber's schema underlies the course of history' (sic). This is pure nonsense, which will probably amuse Troeltsch just as much as anyone who knows what his works are really about – though not those who do not know them, who are the very readers Rachfahl is hoping for. Similarly, in his review, he described von Schulze-Gaevernitz and von Schubert just as disciples of my 'teachings', with my having 'left' the 'Jews' to Sombart, 'as is well known'. So it appears I have a whole army of eminent scholars dancing to my tune. And now presumably Professor H. Levy[xliii] belongs here too after my reference to a friendly note from him, which Rachfahl greets spitefully and childishly as evidence of a 'working party' – and presumably also Professor A. Wahl, whom Rachfahl thinks I 'hardly did a favour' in reporting a remark of his.

Rachfahl shows a similar standard when he pretends to his readers that Troeltsch contradicted or even 'retracted' his *expressly* reiterated agreement with my theses on the psychology of religion – knowing *perfectly well* that wherever Troeltsch agrees with me, he means explicitly or self-evidently my discussion of theological and religious psychology,

---

xliii   Hermann Levy (1881–1949): professor of economics at Heidelberg from 1914. See Part III, Weber's note 13, p.78, in this volume.

which was what my essay specifically dealt with in any depth and of which he is a much better judge than I, being a specialist in the area. Conversely, Rachfahl knows full well that wherever Troeltsch declares himself *not* competent and not a specialist, he obviously does not mean anything falling in his *special* area but rather the economic information I used to illustrate the otherwise well-known fact of ascetic Protestantism's economic supremacy.

9   Where I agree with Rachfahl about the role of tolerance is clear enough in my essay, as I indicated in my previous Reply. Rachfahl has added absolutely nothing new here.

10   A *'fabricator* of history' [*Geschichtskonstrukteur*] might very well get it into his head to derive the uniqueness of the Dutch experience from Calvinism's largely having had to abstain from intolerance here (even though it is least known to have done so in the province of Holland itself). There could even be a grain of truth in this – though certainly only a small one.

On the subject of Holland, I have referred to the fact that Groen van Prinsterer[xliv] mentions the combination of strong profits with limited expenditure as specific to Dutch economic development, just like I did. (Incidentally, we find a graphic picture of Groen's unique attitude to Prussian conservatism and his overridingly religious politics in his correspondence with the Stahl circle,[xlv] whom he closely influenced.) Yet Rachfahl, who does not know this passage (let him look for it to lend depth to his reading!), *doubts* whether I have read this scholar. In any other writer with thicker blood in his veins, I would have to call this an 'impertinence'; but since Rachfahl sees little harm in such practices, I may as well spare myself the effort.

Busken-Huët[xlvi] may have good reason to speak of Erasmus occasionally as a founding father of Dutch culture, given the specific things he discusses in this context. But in a way that is extremely problematic, Rachfahl now 'absolutises' this idea of Erasmus as a founding father both of Holland's *religious* character and of its *economic* peculiarities. Groen van Prinsterer and Busken-Huët would have both laughed, as I now do. Anyone with an open mind for sixteenth- and especially seventeenth-century Dutch history will know how foolish it is to speak of 'the' Dutch culture, as Rachfahl does, in Busken-Huët's name, given the wider concept of 'culture' at issue here. Rather, anyone will know what sharp contradictions have existed side by side with each other in Dutch history, right until today. That this Dutch characteristic Groen takes for granted as a fact had much to do with the strict discipline of the Dutch religious communities will be seen by anyone with any acquaintance with the internal debates of these communities. They were absolutely typical problems of conduct of life – the same problems that arose for the Huguenots and the Pietists and in America; and although different in individual details according to cultural milieu, they were all dealt with in fundamentally the same rigorous way. For all the apparent authority he displays, I would not want to ask Rachfahl to swear to his mastery of this field. For anyone who has worked here can see that he knows *nothing* about it. He is generally ignorant even of the small *fraction* of literature on my topic that I cited in the essay. Perhaps he will try to make up for this. But clearly, to get a decent overview he will need to do far more than what he has managed so far, which amounts to nothing more than a little stroll through other people's works with the schoolmaster's cane in his hand, ready perhaps to rap over the knuckles of the inept non-historian. I for one do not give up hope of continuing and extending these elements of my work. Admittedly, this presupposes

---

[xliv]   See Part III, trans. note xv, p.68, in this volume.

[xlv]   Friedrich Julius Stahl (1802–61): jurist and Lutheran churchman, member of the Prussian parliament from 1849, influential conservative figure and defender of the established state church under the reign of Friedrich Wilhelm IV.

[xlvi]   Conrad Busken-Huët (1826–86): prominent Dutch literary critic, author of *Het Land van Rembrandt* ['Rembrandt's Country'], 1882–84.

another visit to America, as certain documents on Quaker and Baptist history are obtainable only over there. On the continent of Europe, certain things are missing, even from the Dutch libraries. They can only be found in the old sectarian colleges there, or else in England (and even there I am not sure how completely).

Having said all this, Holland also undoubtedly saw a good deal of swanky display and gluttony among its parvenus – quite in contrast to those Pietist circles and ascetic sects. Then there was that naive earthy *Lebensfreude* of the fenland farmers who set the foundations for the capitalism of the towns and generally had it all 'too good' (from the ascetic standpoint). There was the petty bourgeoisie, in part similarly disposed. There was an artistic bohemian group; and finally there were the humanistically educated strata, with refined aesthetic, literary and scientific tastes and judgements. These contrasts, incidentally, were already present in a slightly different form among those Dutch people who migrated north from the southern Netherlands. Such migrants included *not only* political fugitives *without* religious passions but also numerous Calvinists, and also *artists* holding incorrect personal or even artistic views likely to be persecuted or at least disadvantaged by the church. These artists typically led their lives in a way that made it seriously possible to claim they methodically cultivated their dissoluteness 'on principle' – as a kind of negative vocational ethic, a negation of inner-worldly asceticism.

11   Such reductions in the stock of private wealth and population were often of course the result of intolerance, Protestant as much as Catholic (also in Geneva, for example, as I emphasised). However, wealth is not the same as accumulated capital, and population not the same as population with a psychological disposition for capitalism. What was decisive was still the 'spirit' governing the population – and thereby economic life – whether tolerated or not.

12   The first case of this is what he says about 'good Lutheran Hamburg'. Rachfahl objects to what I said about Hamburg and my reference to Adalbert Wahl[xlvii] on the grounds that private fortunes founded on commerce are less secure than those founded on industry (hence Hamburg's difference from Basle). Assuming this thesis to be generally correct (imparted to him, he says, by a 'valued colleague from elsewhere' – presumably the same admirable historian who informed me?),[xlviii] then clearly my reason for citing *this* circumstance is even stronger, namely that apparently the *only* family with a continuous *commercial* fortune since the seventeenth century with the same stability as the Basle *industrial* fortunes is one belonging to the *Reformed* [Calvinist] confession. This is precisely how confessional differences operate. Let me repeat *again* here that I cannot presently check the causal details of this circumstance. It could of course be attributable to numerous 'coincidences'; yet these 'coincidences' considerably *mount up* – to say nothing of the large-scale developmental connections between capitalism and Protestantism I referred to in whole countries. I cited this only because Rachfahl tried to adduce the totally self-evident fact of instances of capitalist development in all ages without ascetic Protestantism as an 'objection' to me.

Rachfahl contends that Petty, quoted by him before me – though quite incompletely of course, i.e. only as far as it suited his 'critique' – was 'not thinking' of capitalists in the passage I quoted – even though Petty's whole discussion starts from the fact that in all Catholic countries *business* was substantially in the hands of heretics, and from the question of why *this* was so (as with so many writings of this period) and in particular whence originated the international economic power of Holland, the origin of that 'capitalistic' prosperity that mercantilism wanted to measure by the amount of money flowing into countries. And the paradoxical aspect of Petty's account lies in *precisely* the problem that I saw and tried to explain without having first paid attention to this passage. I mean the

---

xlvii See Part III, trans. note xiii, p.67, in this volume.
xlviii Rachfahl's text suggests that this was not in fact Wahl but someone else.

problem of how it was that those who became the carriers of that 'spirit' of early modern capitalism, which was no longer based on ethical *laxity*, as in the Middle Ages, were precisely those broad strata of the bourgeois rising middle classes who condemned the wealthy and sinful consumption (see my quotation from Petty above)[xlix] and who *for precisely this reason* maintained a separate religious community with their own lifestyle and a religious vocational ethic. That Petty had the Dutch freedom-fighters in mind, as Rachfahl objects, is once again something I said myself. That Petty looked on these people not as a historian but through the eyes of his *own* time (the seventeenth century) (*now* causing Rachfahl for once to doubt the significance of this writer's statements) thus actually shows that at a time when, by Rachfahl's own thesis, Holland was *no longer* governed by religious motives, the exceptions to this [i.e. those Dutchmen still governed by religious motives, by Calvinism] were well-schooled businessmen. Not all of even Rachfahl's readers will believe I really suffered the 'misfortune' of identifying the Dutch freedom fighters with the English Dissenters observed by Petty. That Dutch heresy at the time of the break with Spain had 'nothing to do' with the later English Dissenters can only be claimed by someone who knows nothing of this matter. Puritan Dissent in England was continually fed and intellectually supported in the strongest way possible by Holland and (as in Holland itself) by fugitives from the southern Netherlands. All the sources of the period indicate this, including the religious trials under Elizabeth. Dutch influences ultimately underlie not only Calvinism's specifically ascetic turn but also the development in the Baptist movement that became so important for the emergence of the Independents (whose literature always claimed and still claims the glory for being the carrier of our specifically modern political–economic principles) and of the Mennonites (whose 'mercantilist' usefulness even induced bellicose Prussian kings to grant exemption from military service). And they also underlie, indirectly, that last efflorescence of adult baptism growing out of the Independents that was Quakerism – whose tradition likewise constantly claims the glory of bequeathing our modern business ethics and hence of being 'blessed by God with property' – and finally also of Pietism. As in New England and Pennsylvania, so in the Netherlands the basic form of the practical vocational ethic had to develop first on relatively little capitalist soil (in East Friesland), and therefore cannot have been a *result* of capitalist development. But then Amsterdam and Leyden became the breeding grounds on which specifically sectarian principles of congregational life were nurtured, which once perfected there then spread to England. Finally it was from Holland that the voyages of the Pilgrim Fathers took their impetus, as our historian ought likewise to know – even if one cannot expect him to be familiar with the Scottish and English Quaker elements and with Dissent in general in England upto the present.

Lastly let me mention Rachfahl's highly misleading interpretation of the statement of Calvin's I quoted (to which, incidentally, I could have added others) when he writes that Calvin *commanded* enjoyment of life 'in respect of the senses'. This also does not prevent him from asserting elsewhere that even Calvin himself upheld principles that became characteristic of ascetic Calvinism and underpinned the growth of the capitalist spirit.

13   See above [in Rachfahl's text, p.90, in this volume]. With someone who quibbles over words like Rachfahl, one has to give references as one does with manuscript documents; for otherwise he cannot find his own assertions. See also above [Rachfahl's text], where he describes my view as a mere 'figure of speech called *pars pro toto*, as we are told at school'. *He*, meanwhile, forgets that he *himself* doubted whether the 'capitalist ethic' concurred in *any sense whatever* with the Calvinist vocational ethic.

[xlix]   Part III: 'These people (the Puritan Dissenters), believing the justice of God ...' etc., see p.68, in this volume.

14   In the case of present-day America, I refer incidentally here to [Thorstein] Veblen's excellent book, *Theory of Business Enterprise* (1904). This book highlights among other things the gradual *emancipation* of the most modern kinds of multi-millionaire from that *bourgeois* mentality characteristic of modern capitalism until now and encapsulated in the maxim: 'honesty is the best policy'. I have examined the genesis of this maxim in my *Archiv* and *Christliche Welt* essays, and return to it below.

15   I am quite unclear about where in Rachfahl's text I am supposed to find any such 'debate' with me about the relation between irrational 'drive' and rational 'spirit'. I refer to my previous Reply and advise Rachfahl to make rather higher demands on himself.

16   Rachfahl complains of my view of the spiteful (in tone) and petty (in content) way he harped on about the example I mentioned (by way of illustration in a footnote in very *few* lines) of a highly successful businessman who continued avoiding certain luxury foods (oysters) even when prescribed them by a doctor, because he possessed that 'ascetic' trait characteristic of whole generations of people that saw pleasurable consumption and luxury in contrast to the proper vocational use of property in the form of capital as 'wrong' *as such*. Rachfahl complains in this way in order to make it seem as though I were depending on such remarks for decisive '*evidence*'. I now find him *still* exploiting this example in the same way *despite* my comments, and even – despite my broad and copious illustrations of the *overall* attitude in which that small trait belongs, next to numerous other traits – *being shameless enough* to tell his readers that he Rachfahl at least has 'not attempted to invoke the modalities of oyster consumption for the purposes of knowledge'. Such writing is 'effective' indeed.

17   According to what suits him, the period that 'matters' for Rachfahl is sometimes the sixteenth century, sometimes the eighteenth century. However, Calvinism's specifically ascetic turn occurred precisely in the seventeenth century and the immediately adjacent years. It was also in this period that the Baptist movement, once it had recovered its reputation after the tumult at Münster,[1] gradually differentiated into Anabaptism, General Baptism and Particular Baptism, in parallel with the rise of Quakerism and Pietism. (Methodism I described as a latecomer and a 'revivalist' movement.) This was also precisely the time of the first large-scale and systematic development of consciously *bourgeois*–capitalist modern politics *and literature*. Thus it is obvious that Rachfahl's dates reflect his quite understandable quandary in trying to uphold an erroneous polemical position at any price.

18   Actually this last imputation seems rather to correspond to the view Rachfahl himself defends in his review – if 'defending a view' is the right term for such self-seeking wrangling. Rachfahl believes that it is Calvinism ('above all else') that tends to 'serve' (sic) 'small and medium-scale traders and craftsmen' and especially administrative employees (sic), as well as the 'workforce' (sic) and the 'capitalists' – a dictum that makes one wonder in vain at what floundering thoughtlessness could have engendered it. Just one case will illustrate how utterly mindlessly Rachfahl conducts himself in this matter. At one point he emits such a cry of triumph that for once, after all his other disgraces, I would really feel like granting him this – if only it stood up to even the most superficial examination. He assures his readers that it is extremely 'unpleasant' for me to be 'nailed down' on my reference to craftsmen traders in New England as evidence of *capitalist spirit*. If his readers were to look for themselves at the passage thus 'nailed down', they would find the following: 'The existence of iron-works (1643), weaving for the market (1659), and also the high development of the handicrafts in New England in the first generation after the

---

[1]   Retaliating against persecution by both Catholic and Protestant rulers and flouting their own teachings on peace, a large number of early Anabaptist followers took over the town of Münster in Westphalia in 1534 by violent means. However, they were soon crushed and their leaders executed.

foundation of the colonies are, from a purely economic viewpoint, *anachronisms*. They are in striking contrast to the conditions in the South ...'[li] I do not of course need to alter one word of this remark. Nor need I change anything of the underlying reasoning that saw, like the Americans before me, how these in part capitalist phenomena and in part strong and independent forms of small-scale industry (which were all the more remarkable for a colonial area still largely at the level of subsistence economy, as Rachfahl has read in my work and occasionally claims for himself against me) were conditioned by the immigrants' overwhelmingly religious lifestyle. So, leaving aside the obvious answer to what has been 'nailed down' here, let *me* now 'nail down' Rachfahl's question: what spirit can have bred a 'review' that sees its business in *nothing more* than trying to 'nail down' the author to individual *words* and *sentences* – and moreover constantly failing? From A to Z, you will find nothing but this in Rachfahl's 'review' and 'reply'.

19   The maxim 'whoever will not work, shall not eat' has been directed against parasitic missions found in every age. We see a classic case of it today in the divine 'call' that tends to assail the Negro who finds existence as a holy man more desirable than as a worker. This has been delightfully portrayed by Booker Washington.[lii] We find other expressions of it in parables, and others have an eschatological cause. One finds a *positive* view of work much more among the Cynics and in a number of pagan Hellenistic grave inscriptions from lower middle-class circles. Considering the comments in my essay about the influence of the Old Testament spirit on the Puritan vocational ethic, I find it rather grotesque of Rachfahl now to present these things as an objection to me when the emptiness of his casual remark reveals that he can only have known about them from my comments. I did also, incidentally, remind the reader of how this Old Testament renascence was connected to the specific characteristics of Puritan religiosity I discussed. Yet this too Rachfahl forgets.

20   This is not intended as a general statement about the possible pedagogical value of confession. One only has to find out what is actually asked about in confession, by examining the instructions for confession or by some other means, to see that these things were and are quite different from those that concern us here. A good example of Catholicism's *practical* attitude to economic life, incidentally, is provided by the history of the ban on usury. As is well known, this ban has still not been rescinded even today; and given the fixed maxims of Catholic church governance, neither can it be – because it is expressly contained in the Decretals. We know the reason for this to lie with a false reading of the Greek (μηδένα instead of μηδὲν ἀπελπίζοντες) in the (inspired!) Vulgate translation.[liii] In practice, however, it has been made inoperative by instructions from the papal curia (although only definitively inoperative for less than a century). These orders are that confessors

---

[li]   PE:278, n.86 [trans. mod]. Note that Parsons misses the point of this remark by translating *Anachronismen* as 'astounding'.

[lii]   Booker T. Washington (1856–1915): spokesman for black Americans, founder of the Tuskegee Institute in 1881 for the education of black people. In his writings and approach to education, Booker Washington typically emphasised hard work and patience and predominantly vocational industrial skills.

[liii]   Weber is referring to the passage in the Gospel according to St. Luke, 6.35: 'But love your enemies, do good, and lend, expecting nothing in return' (πλὴν ἀγαπᾶτε τοὺς ἐχθροὺς ὑμῶν καὶ ἀγαθοποιεῖτε καὶ δαυίζετε μηδὲν ἀπελπίζοντες). The context of this passage necessarily requires the meaning 'expecting nothing in return'. However, this meaning of the verb ἀπελπίζω is unusual and in later Greek it consistently meant 'to despair of'. Consequently, the Vulgate falsely assumed the correct Greek manuscript to read μηδένα ἀπελπίζοντες, with the meaning 'despairing of nobody' (verumtamen diligite inimicos vestros et benefacite et mutuum date nihil desperantes). (Note: In the German, Weber writes 'μηδὲν statt μηδένα', i.e in reverse order to the Greek text cited here. This appears to be an oversight on Weber's part.)

should no longer inquire about *usuraria pravitas* involving transactions with interest, provided it can be assumed the penitent *would* follow obediently *if* the church found it opportune to insist on the ban. (Thus much in the same way as certain public discussions in French Catholic circles prefer confessors not to inquire any longer about *onanismus matrimonialis*, copulation made sterile for the sake of the two-child system, despite the Biblical curse on *coitus interruptus* – discussions so far unchallenged by ecclesiastical censors, as far as I know.) This procedure is thoroughly characteristic of the Catholic church. Just as in the Middle Ages when it *tolerated* the actual existence of the machinery of capitalism without positively *approving* of it in *any* form and without failing to punish certain forms of it [such as the taking of interest], so now, *temporum ratione habita*, it tolerates these forms *too*. Protestant asceticism, on the other hand, created that machinery's positive ethic: it created the 'soul' it needed to unite 'spirit' with 'form'.

21   In my article, I compared this creditworthiness with a German fraternity student's ability to 'live on tick'. (In my time, it was possible for a student to live almost for free in Heidelberg after 'gaining the ribbon' from his fraternity; and if you were a *Fuchs* [new member] you could record your debts with the Registrar.) I also noted a similarly specific creditworthiness of the clergy in the Middle Ages (where the threat of excommunication could be used as a sanction). Similar again is the often dubious creditworthiness of the modern young officer, where the sanction is possible dismissal. However, there is a sociologically highly significant difference here in that, in all these cases, credit worthiness is not demanded as a *subjective* quality of the *personality* like it is in the sects (through selection according to appropriate education). Only certain *objective* guarantees are increased (which is something the sects required in addition). The Methodists' characteristic 'training'[liv] for young people has disappeared but it was once highly significant. The same is true for that characteristic custom of gathering in small groups for regular examination on the state of one's soul, i.e. for a kind of limited public confession. This of course denoted a completely different psychological *situation* from Catholic confession behind the window grille since it involved personal equals grouping together.

22   Educating people to take a prevailing interest in 'real things' is, as I indicated, an old and quite definitely religiously anchored principle of Pietist pedagogy. From the outset, we find something very similar among the Quakers and Baptists; and in the Reformed church it is not uncommon today, for example in the preference for *Realschulen* and other similar types of school and in choice of vocation.[lv] These points are of immense importance for the connection between religious forms and modern capitalist development. The Reformation's familiar achievements *in general* are also undoubtedly significant for elementary school education. However, these last connections had their limits, for the achievements of the Prussian state in elementary education were *not* matched in the country of capitalism's greatest development: England. The 'good elementary school' did *not as such* emerge in parallel with capitalist development. Incidentally, it is a quite dubious exaggeration to say, with Rachfahl, that no anxiety prevails or prevailed in Protestantism about increasing levels of education among ordinary people, especially where our good Protestant landowners east of the Elbe are concerned. In my essay I underlined the connection between certain denominational trends in schooling and the position taken towards *fides implicita*.[lvi]

23   In the denominationally mixed areas of Westphalia, it was quite normal until 30 years ago to find incessant skirmishes between Lutherans and members of the Reformed

---

liv   English in original.

lv   Since Weber's day, German *Realschulen* have tended to emphasise the sciences and technical subjects over the humanities, unlike the *Gymnasien*.

lvi   Fides implicita: implicit faith in all the teachings of the church, even when not properly understood. See Weber 1978b: vol. II, 566.

[Calvinist] church, especially among confirmation candidates. The former were seen as 'dragging the Saviour through the gutter' (i.e. through the intestine – because of the *hoc 'est' corpus meum*), while the latter were viewed as 'hypocritical do-gooders' [*heuchlerische Werkheilige*].

24   The special character of the Lutheran Church of Missouri compared with other denominations has remained very pronounced.

25   It is Rachfahl's character to make the greatest efforts to try and 'discredit' (*this* being all he understands by 'critique') both this term and the corresponding *substantive* thesis about Catholic monasticism's inner affinity to rational asceticism, and then to point out to me that in the opinion of respected church historians these elements of ascetic Protestantism denote a 'not yet' complete overcoming of Catholicism. In this 'yet', however, lurks a developmental *construct*, as well as a subjectively unchallengeable *evaluation* that sees Lutheranism as Protestantism's 'highest' manifestation, just inasmuch as it rejects all work-holiness [*Werkheiligkeit*] – and then builds further stages up from that. *Historically*, however, the development of inner-worldly asceticism is a product of the *post*-Reformation period, and therefore more a *reawakening* of religious motives that Catholicism fostered *too*, though in a very different way and with different effects.

26   As far as the opportunity allowed, I have indicated elsewhere ('Agrarverhältnisse im Altertum')[lvii] how the emergence of 'homo oeconomicus' was limited by quite definite *objective* conditions, and that it was these conditions – geographical, political, social and other – that limited the culture of the Middle Ages, in contrast to antiquity. The causal position of modern science in the factors conditioning economic progress has been explained at length by Sombart.

27   Compare, for example, John Keats's letter to his brother Thomas (3 July 1818): 'These churchmen' have turned Scotland into 'colonies of savers and successful entrepreneurs' (in contrast to Ireland, whence he is writing).

28   However, these forces were not of course crushed by the predominant Arminianism (and even indifference) I mentioned among certain political élites. For just such allegiances are found elsewhere. In Holland it was the upper strata who most often strove (at least partially) to *relinquish* capitalist activity by 'ennobling' their fortunes in manorial estates, like in England. Incidentally, the fact that despite my essay's express comment on Arminianism Rachfahl still took it on himself to describe these widely known matters as unfamiliar to me, and to repeat other points like this after my pointing them out first, only bears out everything I do not want to have to keep on saying about him.

29   Let there be no misunderstanding: this stagnation definitely had certain key political causes, in both foreign and domestic policy. But this should in no way exclude the relevance of that dispersion and fracturing of the ascetic life. Presently I am in no position to answer this question conclusively – and doubtless nor are others.

30   That a number of reputable theological colleagues have *not* received my forays into this with either complete indifference or hostility is a great cause of satisfaction to me. For I completely understand that to them this way of relating certain series of religious motivations to their consequences for civil life must appear not to do justice to the ultimate *value content* of the forms of religiosity in question – since from the standpoint of religious *value-judgement*, these motivations are coarse and external, peripheral to true religious contents for the inwardly religious nature. And indeed, they are right. However, such merely 'sociological' work must *also* be carried out – as it has been done by some of the theologians themselves, pre-eminently by Troeltsch. It should surely be done best by the specialists, to whom we outsiders can just here and there offer possible *perspectives on the problem*, in our way and from our own viewpoint, whether they greet us with approval and

---

lvii   Weber 1909.

interest or not. *This* was what I had hoped to achieve, and it is from quarters such as *these* that I expected fruitful and instructive criticism to come – not from part-timer, dilettante, bungling wranglers such as Rachfahl.

31   This would of course need closer interpretation, which I cannot supply here. Seen in purely objective terms, an entrepreneurial risk, however foolhardy, does not in any way imply an 'adventure' if it forms an integral part of a *rationally* calculated business deal.

32   If one compares his earlier remarks with his present ones, one might well be forgiven for thinking that the latter seem more meant as a sort of 'punishment' for my irreverence than anything else.

Bibliography

Anderson, M.L. (1986) 'The *Kulturkampf* and the Course of German History', *Central European History* 19, 1: 82–115.

Ay, K.-L. (1998) 'Max Weber: A German Intellectual and the Question of War Guilt after the Great War', in S. Whimster (ed.) *Max Weber and the Culture of Anarchy*, Basingstoke: Macmillan.

Badcock, G. D. (1998) *The Way of Life: A Theology of Christian Vocation*, Cambridge, Mass.: William B. Eerdmans.

Barnett, T. (1988) *Sociology and Development*, London: Hutchinson.

Bendix, R. (1960) *Max Weber: An Intellectual Portrait*, London: Heinemann.

Benjamin, W. (1970) 'The Task of the Translator', in *Illuminations*, London: Cape.

Blackbourn, D. (1988) 'Progress and Piety: Liberalism, Catholicism and the State in Imperial Germany', *History Workshop Journal* 26: 57–78.

Bouchard, C.B. (1991) *Holy Entrepreneurs: Cistercians, Knights and Economic Exchange in Twelfth Century Burgundy*, Ithaca: Cornell University Press.

Bouma, G. (1973) 'Beyond Lenski: A Critical Review of Recent "Protestant Ethic" Research', reprinted (1991) in P. Hamilton (ed.) *Max Weber (1) Critical Assessments: Volume 2*, London: Routledge.

Brentano, L. (1916) *Die Anfänge des Modernen Kapitalismus*, Munich.

Chalcraft, D.J. (1992) 'Max Weber's Protestant Ethic: A Critical Textual Analysis', unpublished Master of Letters thesis, University of Oxford.

—— (1993) 'Weber, Wagner and Thoughts of Death', *Sociology* 27, 3: 433–49.

—— (1994) 'Bringing the Text Back In: On Ways of Reading the Iron Cage Metaphor in the Two Editions of *The Protestant Ethic*', in L. Ray and M. Reed (eds) *Organizing Modernity*, London: Routledge.

—— (1998) 'Love and Death: Weber, Wagner and Max Klinger', in S. Whimster (ed.) *Max Weber and the Culture of Anarchy*, Basingstoke: Macmillan.

—— (2000a) 'Lifting the Veil on Max Weber's Symbolist Imagination', unpublished paper presented to the Centre for Social Research Seminar Series, University of Derby, April.

133

Bibliography

—— (2000b) 'Max Weber Studies Today', *Self, Agency and Society* 2.2: 105–20.

—— (2000c) 'Max Weber on the Watchtower: Prophetic Uses of Shakespeare's Sonnet 102 in "Politics as a Vocation"', *Centre for Social Research Working Papers*, Series 2, No. 1, University of Derby.

—— (2001a) 'Weber Studies: Division and Interdependence', *History of the Human Sciences*, 14, 1: 105–18.

—— (2001b) 'On the Derivation of the Polar Night of Icy Darkness and Hardness in Weber's Politics a a Vocation', *Max Weber Studies*, issue 2 (forthcoming).

—— (2001c) 'The Lamentable Chain of Misunderstanding; A Critical and Linguistic Analysis of Weber's Debate with H. Karl Fisher', *Self, Agency and Society*, 3, 2 (forthcoming).

—— (2001d) 'The Cultural Significance of the Consumption of Oysters: Max Weber and Felix Rachfahl's Debate on the Meaning of Asceticism and the Spirit of Capitalism', *Max Weber Studies* (forthcoming).

Clegg, S.R. (1990) *Modern Organizations: Organization Studies in the Postmodern World*, London: Sage.

—— (1994) 'Max Weber and the Contemporary Sociology of Organizations', in L. Ray and M. Reed (eds) *Organizing Modernity*, London: Routledge.

Cohen, J. (1980) 'Rational Capitalism in Renaissance Italy', *American Journal of Sociology* 85, 6: 1340–55.

—— (1983) 'Reply to Holton', *American Journal of Sociology* 89, 1: 181–87.

Collins, R. (1986) *Weberian Sociological Theory* Cambridge: Cambridge University Press.

Davis, W.M. (1978) 'Introduction to Max Weber: Anticritical Last Word on The Spirit of Capitalism', *American Journal of Sociology* 83, 5: 1105–10.

Fischer, H.K. (1907) 'Kritische Beiträge zu Professor Max Webers Abhandlung "Die protestantische Ethik und der Geist des Kapitalismus"', reprinted (1978) in J. Winckelmann (ed.) *Max Weber: Die protestantische Ethik II: Kritiken und Antikritiken*, Gütersloh: Gütersloher Verlagshaus.

—— (1908) 'Protestantische Ethik und "Geist des Kapitalismus": Replik auf Herrn Professor Max Webers Gegenkritik', reprinted (1978) in J. Winckelmann (ed.) *Max Weber: Die protestantische Ethik II: Kritiken und Antikritiken*, Gütersloh: Gütersloher Verlagshaus.

—— (2000) 'Two Critiques of Max Weber's "The Protestant Ethic and the Spirit of Capitalism"', ed. D.J. Chalcraft, trans. M. Shields, University of Derby Centre for Social Research Working Papers (forthcoming).

Fischoff, E. (1944) 'The Protestant Ethic and the Spirit of Capitalism: The History of a Controversy', reprinted (1991) in P. Hamilton (ed.) *Max Weber (1) Critical Assessments: Volume 2*, London: Routledge.

Forster, M. (1997) *Rich Desserts and Captain's Thins: A Family and their Times 1831–1931*, London: Vintage.

Frommer, S. and Frommer J. (1990) 'Der Begriff des psychologischen Verstehens bei Max Weber', *Psychologie und Geschichte* 2, 1: 37–44.

Furnham, A. (1990) *The Protestant Work Ethic: The Psychology of Work-Related Beliefs and Behaviour*, London: Routledge.

Gay, P. d. (2000) *In Praise of Bureaucracy: Weber. Organization. Ethics*, London: Sage.

Gellner, E. (1988) *Plough, Sword and Book: The Structure of Human History*, London: Paladin.

Ghosh, P. (1994) 'Some Problems with Talcott Parsons' Version of '*The Protestant Ethic*', *Archives Européennes de Sociologie* 35: 104–23.

Goldman, H. (1988) *Max Weber and Thomas Mann. The Calling and the Shaping of the Self*, Berkeley: University of California Press.

Gorski, P.S. (1993) '*The Protestant Ethic* Revisited: Disciplinary Revolution and State Formation in Holland and Prussia', *American Journal of Sociology* 99, 2: 265–316.

Gothein, E. (1892) *Wirtschaftsgeschichte des Schwarzwaldes*, Strasbourg: Trübner.

Greyerz, K.v. (1993) 'Biographical Evidence on Predestination, Covenant, and Special Providence', in H. Lehmann and G. Roth (eds) *Weber's Protestant Ethic: Origins, Evidence, Contexts*, Cambridge: Cambridge University Press.

Grint, K. (1991) *The Sociology of Work: An Introduction*, Cambridge: Polity Press.

Hamilton, M. (1995) *The Sociology of Religion: Theoretical and Comparative Perspectives*, London: Routledge.

Hanyu, T. (1994) 'Max Webers Quellenbehandlung in der 'Protestantischen Ethik': Der Berufsbegriff', *Archives Européennes de Sociologie* 35, 4: 72–101.

Harrington, A. (2000) 'In Defence of Verstehen and Erklären: Wilhelm Dilthey's "Ideas Concerning a Descriptive and Analytical Psychology"', *Theory and Psychology* 10, 4: 435–51.

—— (2001) 'Empathy and Verstehen: The Early Dilthey', in *Hermeneutic Dialogue and Social Science: A Critique of Gadamer and Habermas*, London: Routledge.

Harrison, D. (1988) *The Sociology of Modernization and Development*, London: Unwin Hyman.

Hennis, W. (1988) *Max Weber: Essays in Reconstruction*, trans. K. Tribe, London. Allen & Unwin.

Hernes, G. (1989) 'The Logic of the Protestant Ethic', *Rationality and Society* 1: 123–162.

Hinkle, G.J. (1986) 'The Americanisation of Max Weber', *Current Perspectives in Social Theory* 7: 87–104.

Holton, R.J. (1983) 'Max Weber, "Rational Capitalism", and Renaissance Italy: A Critique of Cohen', *American Journal of Sociology* 89, 1: 166–180.

Hughes, J. (1986) *The Vital Few. The Entrepreneur and American Economic Progress*, 2nd enlarged edition, Oxford: Oxford University Press.

Jameson, F. (1974) 'The Vanishing Mediator: Narrative Structure in Max Weber', *New German Critique* 1:52–89.

Jones, H.B. (1997) 'The Protestant Ethic: Weber's Model and the Empirical Literature', *Human Relations* 50, 7: 757–78.

Kaesler, D. (1988) *Max Weber: An Introduction to His Life and Work*, Cambridge: Polity Press.

Keeter, L. (1981) 'Max Weber's Visit to North Carolina', *The Journal of the History of Sociology* 3, 2:108–14.

Lehmann, H. (1993) 'The Rise of Capitalism: Weber versus Sombart', in H. Lehmann and G. Roth (eds) *Weber's Protestant Ethic: Origins, Evidence, Contexts*, Cambridge: Cambridge University Press.

Lepsius, R. (1977) 'Max Weber in München: Rede anläßlich der Enthüllung einer Gedanktafel', *Zeitschrift für Soziologie* 6, 1:91–118.

Bibliography

Lichtblau, K. and Weiss, J. (1993) 'Einleitung der Herausgeber', in *Max Weber: Die protestantische Ethik und der "Geist" des Kapitalismus. Textausgabe auf der Grundlage der Fassung von 1904/5*, Bodenheim: Athenaeum Hain Hanstein.

Mackinnon, M.H. (1988) 'Part I: Calvinism and the Infallible Assurance of Grace', and 'Part II: Weber's Exploration of Calvinism', *British Journal of Sociology* 39: 143–210.

—— (1993) 'The Longevity of the Thesis: A Critique of the Critics', in H. Lehmann and G. Roth (eds) *Weber's Protestant Ethic: Origins, Evidence, Contexts*, Cambridge: Cambridge University Press.

Malcolmson, C. (1999) *Heart Work: George Herbert and the Protestant Ethic*. Stanford: Stanford University Press.

Marshall, G. (1980) *Presbyteries and Profit: Calvinism and the Development of Capitalism in Scotland, 1560–1707*, Oxford: Oxford University Press.

—— (1982) *In Search of the Spirit of Capitalism. As essay on Max Weber's Protestant Ethic Thesis*, London: Hutchinson.

McAleer, K. (1994) *Dueling: The Cult of Honour in Fin de Siècle Germany*, Princeton, NJ: Princeton University Press.

Münch, P. (1993) 'The Thesis Before Weber: An Archaeology', in H. Lehmann and G. Roth (eds) *Weber's Protestant Ethic: Origins, Evidence, Contexts*, Cambridge: Cambridge University Press.

Oakes, G. (1988) 'Farewell to the *Protestant Ethic*?', *Telos* 78:81–94.

—— (1989) 'Four Questions Concerning *The Protestant Ethic*', *Telos* 81:77–86.

—— (1993) 'The Thing that would not Die: Notes on Refutation', in H. Lehmann and G. Roth (eds) *Weber's Protestant Ethic: Origins, Evidence, Contexts*, Cambridge: Cambridge University Press.

Pellicani, L. (1988) 'Weber and the Myth of Calvinism', *Telos* 75:57–85.

—— (1989) 'Reply to Oakes', *Telos* 81:63–76.

Piccone, P. (1988) 'Rethinking Protestantism, Capitalism and a Few Other things', *Telos* 78:95–108.

Prades, J.A. (1969) *La Sociologie de la Religion chez Max Weber: Essai d'Analyse et de Critique de la Méthode*, Louvain: Editions Nauwelaerts.

Rachfahl, F. (1909) 'Kalvinismus und Kapitalismus', reprinted (1978) in J. Winckelmann (ed.) *Max Weber: Die protestantische Ethik II: Kritiken und Antikritiken*, Gütersloh: Gütersloher Verlagshaus.

—— (1910) 'Nochmals Kalvinismus und Kapitalismus', reprinted (1978) in J. Winckelmann (ed.) *Max Weber: Die protestantische Ethik II: Kritiken und Antikritiken*, Gütersloh: Gütersloher Verlagshaus.

Ray, L. (1987) 'The Protestant Ethic Debate', in R.J. Andersen, J.A. Hughes and W.W. Sharrock (eds), *Classic Disputes in Sociology*, London: Allen & Unwin.

Reisebrodt, M. (1989) 'From Patriarchialism to Capitalism: The Theoretical Context of Max Weber's Agrarian Studies, 1892–93', in K. Tribe (ed.) *Reading Weber*. London: Routledge.

Roberts, R. (1995) (ed.) *Religion and the Transformations of Capitalism*, London: Routledge.

Rossi, P. (1994) 'Weber, Dilthey und Husserls Logische Untersuchungen', in G. Wagner and H. Zipprian (eds) *Max Weberswissenschaftslehre: Interpretation und Kritik*, Frankfurt am Main: Suhrkamp.

Roth, G. (1992) 'Zur Entstehungs- und Wirkungsgeschichte von Max Webers "Protestantische Ethik": Kommentar zur Faksimile-Ausgabe von 1905', in *Vademecum zu einem Klassiker der Geschichte ökonomischer Rationalität*, Düsseldorf: Verlag Wirtschaft und Finanzen.

—— (1993) 'Weber the Would-be Englishman', in H. Lehmann and G. Roth (eds) *Weber's Protestant Ethic: Origins, Evidence, Contexts*, Cambridge: Cambridge University Press.

Samuelson, K. (1961) *Religion and Economic Action*, Stockholm and London: Scandinavian University Books/William Heinemann.

Schluchter, W. (1981) *The Rise of Western Rationalism: Weber's Developmental History*, Berkeley: University of California Press.

—— (1989) *Rationalism, Religion and Domination: A Weberian Perspective*, Berkeley: University of California Press.

Schroeder, H.C. (1995) 'Max Weber und der Puritanismus', *Geschichte und Gesellschaft* 21: 59–78.

Schroeder, R. (1992) *Max Weber and the Sociology of Culture*, London: Sage.

Scott, A. (1997) 'Modernity's Machine Metaphor', *British Journal of Sociology* 48, 4:561–75.

Sharpe, K. (1992) *The Personal Rule of Charles I*, New Haven: Yale University Press.

Shields, M. (1998) 'Max Weber and German Expressionism', in S. Whimster (ed.) *Max Weber and the Culture of Anarchy*, Basingstoke: Macmillan.

Sica, A. (1984) 'The Unknown Max Weber: A Note on Missing Translations', *Mid-American Review of Sociology* 9, 2:3–25.

Silber, I. (1993) 'Monasticism and the 'Protestant Ethic': asceticism, rationality and wealth in the Medieval West', *British Journal of Sociology* 44, 1:103–23.

Simmel, G. (1911) 'Das Abendteuer', in *Philosophische Kultur*, Leipzig: Kröner; trans. (1971) 'The Adventurer', in D. Levine (ed.) *Simmel: On Individuality and Social Forms*, Chicago: Chicago University Press.

Smith, J. (1981) 'The Protestant Ethic Controversy', unpublished Ph.D. thesis, University of Cambridge.

Sombart, W. (1902) *Der moderne Kapitalismus*, Leipzig.

—— (1909) 'Der kapitalistische Unternehmer', *Archiv für Sozialwissenschaft und Sozialpolitik* 29: 689–758.

—— (1913) *Der Bourgeois: zur Geistesgeschichte des modernen Wirtschaftsmenschen*, Munich and Leipzig: Duncker and Humboldt; trans. (1915) *The Quintessence of Capitalism: a Study of the History and Psychology of the Modern Business Man*, London: Fischer Unwin.

Stachniewski, J. (1991) *The Persecutory Imagination. English Puritanism and the Literature of Religious Despair*, Oxford: Oxford University Press.

Swatos, W.H. (1982) 'Sects and Success: Missverstehen in Mount Airy', *Sociological Analysis* 43, 4:375–80.

—— (1998) 'The Protestant Ethic Thesis', in W.H. Swatos (ed.) *Encyclopedia of Religion and Society*, Walnut Creek: Altamira Press.

Tenbruck, F.H. (1989) 'The Problem of Thematic Unity in the Work of Max Weber', in K. Tribe (ed.) *Reading Weber*, London: Routledge.

Thomas, J. (1998) 'Max Weber's Estate: Reflections on Wilhelm Hennis' *Max Webers Wissenschaft vom Menschen*', *History of the Human Sciences* 11, 8:121–28.

Tribe, K. (1988) 'Translator's Introduction', in W. Hennis, *Max Weber Essays in Reconstruction*, London: Allen & Unwin.

—— (1989) 'Introduction', in K. Tribe (ed.) *Reading Weber*, London: Routledge.

Troeltsch, E. (1906a) Protestantisches Christentum und Kirche in der Neuzeit', in P. Hinneberg (ed.) *Die Kultur der Gegenwart I, 4: Die christliche Religion*, Berlin and Leipzig.

—— (1906b) 'Die Bedeutung des Protestantismus für die Entstehung der modernen Welt', *Historische Zeitschrift* 97:1–66; trans. (1958) *Protestantism and Progress*, New York: Beacon Press.

—— (1910) 'Die Kulturbedeutung des Calvinismus', *Internationale Wochenschrift für Wissenschaft, Kunst und Technik* 1910, 4:449–68, 501–08; reprinted (1978) in J. Winckelmann (ed.) *Max Weber: Die protestantische Ethik II: Kritiken und Antikritiken*, Gütersloh: Gütersloher Verlagshaus.

Turner, S.P. (1985) 'Explaining Capitalism: Weber on and against Marx', in R.J. Antonio and R.M. Glassman (eds) *A Weber–Marx Dialogue*, Lawrence: University Press of Kansas.

Tyrell, H. (1990) 'Worum geht es in der 'Protestantischen Ethik ? Ein Versuch zum besseren Veständnis Max Webers', *Saeculum* 41, 2:130–77.

van Duelman, R. (1988) 'Protestantism and Capitalism: Weber's Thesis in Light of Recent Social History', *Telos* 78: 71–80.

Valeri, M. (1997) 'Religion, Discipline and Economy in Calvin's Geneva', *Sixteenth Century Journal* 28, 1:123–42.

Volf, M. (1991) *Work in the Spirit: Toward a Theology of Work*, Oxford: Oxford University Press.

Weber, Alfred (1909) *Über den Standorten der Industrien: Reine Theorien des Standorts*; trans. C.J. Friedrich (1929) *Theory of the Location of Industries*, Chicago: Chicago University Press.

Weber, Marianne (1988) *Max Weber: A Biography*, trans. H. Zohn, with a new introduction by G. Roth, New Brunswick: Transaction.

Weber, Max (1904) 'Die "Objektivität" sozialwissenschaftlicher und sozialpolitischer Erkenntnis', reprinted (1968) in J. Winckelmann (ed.) *Max Weber: Gesammelte Aufsätze zur Wissenschaftslehre*, Tübingen: J.C.B. Mohr/Paul Siebeck; trans. (1949) '"Objectivity" in Social Science and Social Policy', in E. Shils and H. Finch (eds) *Max Weber: The Methodology of the Social Sciences*, New York: Macmillan.

—— (1905) 'Die protestantische Ethik und der "Geist" des Kapitalismus', *Archiv für Sozialwissenschaft und Sozialpolitik* 20:1–54; and 21:1–110.

—— (1905a) 'Roscher und Knies und die logischen Probleme der historischen Nationalökonomie', reprinted (1968) in J. Winkelmann (ed.) *Max Weber: Gesammelte Aufsätze zur Wissenschaftslehre*, Tübingen: J.C.B. Mohr/Paul Siebeck; trans. G. Oakes (1975) *Roscher and Knies: the Logical Problems of Historical Economics*, London: Macmillan.

—— (1906a) 'Kirchen und "Sekten"', *Frankfurter Zeitung* 50, 104, 1 (13 April and 15 April).

—— (1906b) 'Kirchen und "Sekten" in Nordamerika: Eine kirchliche und sozialpolitische Skizze, *Die christliche Welt* 20, 24:558–62 and 20, 25:577–83; trans. (1985) 'Churches and Sects in North America', *Sociological Theory* 3:7–13.

—— (1907) 'Kritische Bemerkungen zu den vorstehenden "Kritischen Beiträgen"', in *Archiv für Sozialwissenschaft und Sozialpolitik* 25:243–49; reprinted (1978) in J. Winckelmann (ed.) *Max Weber: Die protestantische Ethik II: Kritiken und Antikritiken*, Gütersloh: Gütersloher Verlagshaus.

—— (1908a) 'Bemerkungen zu der vorstehenden Replik', in *Archiv für Sozialwissenschaft und Sozialpolitik* 26:275–83; reprinted (1978) in J. Winckelmann (ed.) *Max Weber: Die protestantische Ethik II: Kritiken und Antikritiken*, Gütersloh: Gütersloher Verlagshaus.

—— (1908b) 'Zur Psychophysik der industriellen Arbeit', reprinted (1995) in W. Schluchter (ed.), *Max-Weber-Gesamtausgabe*, I, II, Tübingen: J.C.B. Mohr/Paul Siebeck.

—— (1909) 'Agrarverhältnisse im Altertum', in *Handwörterbuch der Staatswissenschaften* 1; trans. R. Frank (1976) *The Agrarian Sociology of Ancient Civilisations*, London: Humanities Press.

—— (1910a) 'Antikritisches zum "Geist" des Kapitalismus', in *Archiv für Sozialwissenschaft und Sozialpolitik* 30:176–202; reprinted (1978) in J. Winckelmann (ed.) *Max Weber: Die protestantische Ethik II: Kritiken und Antikritiken*, Gütersloh: Gütersloher Verlagshaus.

—— (1910b) 'Antikritisches Schlußwort zum "Geist des Kapitalismus"', in *Archiv für Sozialwissenschaft und Sozialpolitik* 31:554–99; reprinted (1978) in J. Winckelmann (ed.) *Max Weber: Die protestantische Ethik II: Kritiken und Antikritiken*, Gütersloh: Gütersloher Verlagshaus.

—— (1915a) 'Die Wirtschaftsethik der Weltreligionen: Religionssoziologische Skizzen: Einleitung; Der Konfuzianismus I, II', *Archiv für Sozialwissenschaft und Sozialpolitik* 41, 1: 1–87.

—— (1915b) 'Die Wirtschaftsethik der Weltreligionen: Der Konfuzianismus III, IV (Schluss); Zwischenbetractung: Stufen und Richtungen der religiösen Weltablehnungen', *Archiv für Sozialwissenschaft und Sozialpolitik* 41, 2:335–421.

—— (1920) 'Die Protestantische Ethik und der Geist der Kapitalismus', in *Gesammelte Aufsätze zur Religionssoziologie*, vol. I, Tübingen: J.C.B. Mohr/Paul Siebeck.

—— (1930) *The Protestant Ethic and the Spirit of Capitalism*, trans. T. Parsons, London: Unwin Hyman.

—— (1948) *From Max Weber: Essays in Sociology*, ed. H. Gerth and C.W. Mills, London: Routledge.

—— (1949) *Max Weber: The Methodology of the Social Sciences*, ed. E. Shils and H. Finch, New York: Macmillan.

—— (1951) *The Religion of China*, trans. H. Gerth, New York: The Free Press.

—— (1952) *Ancient Judaism*, trans. H. Gerth and D. Martindale, Glencoe, IL: The Free Press.

—— (1958) *The Religion of India*, Glencoe, IL: The Free Press.

—— (1978a) 'Anti-Critical Last Word on the Spirit of Capitalism', trans. W. Davis, *American Journal of Sociology* 83:1105–31.

—— (1978b) *Economy and Society*, ed. G. Roth and C. Wittich, Berkeley: University of California Press.

—— (1981) *General Economic History*, New Brunswick: Transaction.

Bibliography

—— (1990) Letters 1906–08, in R. Lepsius and W. Mommsen (eds) *Max Weber Gesamtausgabe* II, 5, Tübingen: J.C.B. Mohr/Paul Siebeck.

Whimster, S. and Lash, S. (1987) (eds) *Max Weber: Rationality and Modernity*. London. Allen and Unwin.

Wilson, B. (1982) *Religion in Sociological Perspective*, Oxford: Oxford University Press.

Winckelmann, J. (1978) (ed.) *Max Weber: Die protestantische Ethik II, Kritiken und Antikritiken*, Gütersloh: Gütersloher Verlagshaus.

Zaret, D. (1993) 'The Use and Abuse of Textual Data', in H. Lehmann and G. Roth (eds) *Weber's Protestant Ethic: Origins, Evidence, Contexts*, Cambridge: Cambridge University Press.

Index

absolution 6
abstinence 55
academic discussion 9
accusations 9
acquisition economies 76
acquisition of money 35, 65, 72, 78n.6,
    84n.xlix
acquisitive drive (*Erwerbsbetrieb*)
    71–73, 76, 85n.32, 103–104
acquisitiveness 55
adaptation 28, 37n.3, 42, 48n.1
adventurers 119
adventures 132n.31
affinity 13
agonistic drives 83n.31
Agrarverhältnisse im Altertum Max
    Weber 85n.34, 131n.26
agricultural capitalism 79n.14
Alberti, L. B. 6
Althoff, F. 61n.iii
America 8, 89
    see also New England; North
        Carolina
    Puritanism 90, 104
    settlers 79n.14
    Weber's visit 3
American capitalism 57
American democracy 112, 113,
    123–24n.3

Amsterdam 57, 80n.14
Anabaptism 128n.17
Anabaptists 37n.4, 128n.1
ancient world 79n.14
Arminianism 33n.x, 79n.14, 80n.xxxv,
    81n.18, 90, 131n.28
ascetic spirit 83n.31
asceticism 14, 56
    see also inner-worldly asceticism;
        Protestant asceticism
    and calculativeness 91
    and Calvinism 62, 90, 113, 128n.17
    Catholic 56, 65
    concepts 63–65
    in England 82n.24
    minority following 81n.14
    monastic 113–15
    and Protestantism 90
Austria 59
Author's Introduction 4, 5
Avenarius, R. 63n.v

Baptism 32, 37n.xix, 109, 111,
    128n.17, 130n.22
Baptist movement 37n.3, 50n.6
Baptists 28, 32n.vii, 79n.14, 101, 111
Basle 67, 126n.12
Baudelaire, C. 13, 80n.14, 80n.xxxii
Bavaria 4

Index

Index

Puritanism 82n.24, 90, 117
  tolerance 59
Enlightenment 59, 89, 101
enterprise/s 31, 32, 37n.xviii, 50n.5
entrepreneurialism 10, 83n.28, 84n.32,
  101, 116
epistemological standpoint 42
Erasmian humanism 80n.xxxv
Erasmus 91, 125n.10
ethical training 110
Europe 9
evidence 14
exercise 114
expenditure 125n.10
expressionism 13

facts 49n.3, 98
Faraday, M. 120
fate of humanity 12
feelings 29
fencing 13, 16–19
financiers 69, 79n.14
Fischer, H. K. 7, 14–16
fixed prices system 111
Flanders 45
Florence 28, 112
Florentine bourgeoisie 49n.2
France 36, 56
Franck, S. 7, 63, 63n.vii, 114
Frankfurter Zeitung 3
Franklin, B. 6, 9, 14, 69n.xvii, 72,
  76n.xxv
  and J. Fugger 9, 31, 79n.14
  and the spirit of capitalism 31,
    31n.ii/iii, 75, 79n.14
Friesland 37n.3
frugality 55
Fugger, J.
  and the acquisition of money 35
  and Benjamin Franklin 9, 31,
    79n.14
  commercial daring 69n.xvii
  and the conduct of life 57, 78n.7, 81
  and the spirit of capitalism 31n.ii

generalisations 46
Geneva 49n.1, 58

Genoa 28
Germany 117
*Gesammelte Aufsätze zur
  Religionssoziologie* 3, 4
Gnesio-Lutherans 65n.ix
Gothein, E. 37n.xx, 117, 122n.2,
  122n.xxxix
Groen van Prinsterer, G. 68n.xv, 91,
  125n.10
Gymnasien 130n.lv

Hamburg 7, 58, 67, 122n.2, 126n.12
Handwörterbuch der Staatswissenschaft
  Max Weber 85n.37, 119
Harnack, A. von 108n.xvii
Hennis, W. 11–13, 19
heretics 67, 99, 126n.12
hermeneutics 13, 14
historians 2
historical materialism 50n.5, 83n.30,
  95
historical psychology 14–16
historical research 42, 47
Holland
  see also Amsterdam; Arminianism
    and under Dutch
  Calvinism in 9, 33n.ix, 80n.xxxiv,
    125n.10, 127n.12
  capitalist development in 28, 59, 90,
    122n.2, 125n.10
    stagnation of 118, 131n.29
  economic power 126n.12
  Huguenots 117
  middle classes 33n.x, 126n.12
  Protestant asceticism 33n.x, 126n.12
  Puritan dissent 127n.12
  religion 90–91
  tolerance 59, 68
  vocational ethic 126–27n.12
  wealth 56, 68
homo oeconomicus 131n.26
Huguenots 36, 56, 79n.14, 89, 117,
  123n.3
  Edict of Nantes 99n.6
  human rights 123n.3
Humiliati 99n.viii
Hungary 34, 34n.xii, 79n.14

Protestants 113
Providence 116
psycho-speak 16
psychological interpretations 27, 28,
    42, 46
  conduct of life 35, 36
psychological research 42
psychological sanction 6
psychologists 8, 47
psychology 9, 44n.i
  of acquisition 72
  of entrepreneurialism 84n.32
  and historical reality 35, 35n.xiv,
    36–37, 44, 47–48
  reflective (*Reflexionspsychologie*) 13,
    14–16, 29
  of religion 47, 124n.8
puns 70n.xviii
Puritan dissent 127n.12
Puritan personality 12
Puritan Yankee spirit 79n.14
Puritanism
  in America 90, 104
  and conduct of life 34n.xi, 41
  in England 82n.24, 90, 117
  and the middle classes 68
  and soul 12
  vocational ethic 58
Puritans 36, 76, 83n.28/30, 101
putting-out system 37n.xviii

Quakerism 78n.14, 127n.12, 127n.17,
    130n.22
Quakers 79n.14,, 101, 111, 113

Rachfahl, F.
  career and publications 7
  use of *Mensur* in exchanges with
    Weber 16–19
Rathenau, W. 83n.xiv
rationalisation 4, 11–12, 50n.5, 66,
    91
rationality 1
Realschulen 130n.22, 130n.lv
reflective psychology
    (*Reflexionspsychologie*) 13,
    14–16, 29

Reformation 29, 64, 120
  and capitalism 32, 45, 89
  and capitalist spirit 89
  and elementary school education
    130n.22
  and vocational ethic 70, 91
Regensburg, B. von 108
religious ideas 34n.xiii
religious movements 44
religious training 112
Rembrandt 80n.14
Renaissance 57, 120
Renaissance man 36
Renaissance trader 12
renunciation 56
Replies 6, 7
  Archiv sources 23
  history in the PE Debate 9
  Pellicani-Oakes debate 10
  Wilhelm Hennis 11–13
research 13–14, 42, 47
responsibility 78n.6
Rhineland 28
Rhode Island 78n.14
Ritschl, A. 63n.vi
Rockefeller, J. D. 84n.31, 84n.xlix
Roman church 67
Rubens, Peter Paul 80n.14
Russian sects 33

salvation 36, 109, 115
Sandeman, R. 120n.xxxiv
saving 103–104, 116
Schmidt, F. J. 121n.2
scholarship 10
Schulze-Gaevernitz, G. von 121n.2,
    121n.xxxvi
science 120, 131n.26
scientific psychology 47
scientific rationalism 120
Scotland 117, 131n.27
sectarians 8
sects 64, 77
  in American democracy 112
  ascetic 77n.3, 110
  essay on 3, 7
  function in economic life 111

147

Index